Accountant's Audit Guide
for Small and Medium-Sized
Businesses

Accountant's Audit Guide
for Small and Medium-Sized
Businesses

-
-
-
-
-
-
-

Frank

P.

Walker

-
-
-
-
-
-

PRENTICE-HALL, INC.   ENGLEWOOD CLIFFS, N. J.

PRENTICE-HALL INTERNATIONAL, INC., *London*
PRENTICE-HALL OF AUSTRALIA, PTY., LTD., *Sydney*
PRENTICE-HALL OF CANADA, LTD., *Toronto*
PRENTICE-HALL OF INDIA PRIVATE LTD., *New Delhi*
PRENTICE-HALL OF JAPAN, INC., *Tokyo*

© 1970, BY

PRENTICE-HALL, INC.
Englewood Cliffs, N. J.

LIBRARY OF CONGRESS
CATALOG CARD NUMBER: 75-121727

Second Printing.....May, 1972

PRINTED IN THE UNITED STATES OF AMERICA
ISBN-0-13-001024-3
B&P

To my lovely wife Frances in appreciation for her encouragement, patience, and very competent typing.

About the Author

Frank P. Walker:

Native of St. Joseph, Missouri; graduated (A.B.) Rollins College, Winter Park, Florida. Received Certified Public Accountant certificate (by examination) Illinois, 1942. Employed as staff accountant Lybrand, Ross Bros. & Montgomery in Rockford, Illinois for three years, then by Pollard & Wheeler, CPAs; served in the U.S. Navy during World War II (receiving permanent commission as LCDR, Supply Corps, USNR) as accounting officer, NAS Grosse Isle, Michigan, and later in England and Germany.

Controller, later Vice-President, Sales, Elco Corporation, Rockford, Illinois. During this period established cost system, supervised installation EDP system, responsible for establishing and operating profit sharing investment and accounting fund. Resigned in 1959 to move to Arizona, establishing a Certified Public Accounting practice as sole practitioner. In 1969 accepted position as Associate Professor of Accounting at Thunderbird Graduate School of International Management (formerly American Institute for Foreign Trade), Phoenix, Arizona, while continuing public accounting practice on a consulting basis.

During the period of public accounting practice, performed many audits of businesses in the small to medium-size range. (In this connection "medium-sized" might be considered to be those with annual sales up to $25,000,000 or total assets up to $5,000,000, although admittedly these amounts are rather arbitrary.) Consulted frequently with bankers and other financial personnel on behalf of clients seeking loans. Was and is an active member of the Illinois and Arizona CPA Society committees on Cooperation with Bankers and Other Credit Grantors.

Author of articles on accounting subjects in Journal of Accountancy *and state society magazine.*

Audit Guide for Accountants

The attest function of the public accountant is extremely important because by expressing his accountant's opinion, the accountant incurs a responsibility—and a legal liability—to unknown third parties. Over the years, the courts have tended to increase the liability of the accountant expressing an opinion on the financial statements of his clients, and with this increasing responsibility, the public accountant is more than ever on notice to conduct his audit in accordance with accepted auditing principles and procedures so that his opinion will stand the test of professional proficiency.

The large accounting firms, particularly those operating on a national and international level, as well as firms specializing in preparing various financial reports for submission to the Securities and Exchange Commission, have developed auditing manuals designed for use by their staff. These manuals, however, are seldom available to the accounting firms who consistently audit small and medium-sized clients, and even when available are seldom appropriate for use in auditing the records of clients of this size.

Many of the medium, and even small-sized clients, may be engaged in interstate commerce, which often raises some thorny questions as to necessity to register in other states (a problem for the attorney), and to pay additional taxes (a problem for the auditor).

The objective of this book is to present in a concise form procedures particularly designed for use in auditing the records of small and medium-sized organizations. It is not intended as a definitive discussion of the theory and practice of auditing, but, on the contrary, is meant to be a working manual for the daily use of staff auditors and supervisors, which will facilitate the audit and help to avoid the omission of any essential auditing procedure.

It is assumed that the auditor is familiar with "Statements on Auditing Procedure" issued by the Committee on Auditing Procedure of the American Institute of Certified Public Accountants, as well as the "Opinions of the Accounting Principles Board," issued by the Accounting Principles Board of the American Institute of Certified Public Accountants. Since these constitute the most authoritative guidelines available, reference will be made in the text to these statements and opinions. It is further assumed that the accountant is familiar generally with the requirements for the proper preparation of income tax returns for the Internal Revenue Service and for any state which may be involved.

At the same time it must be recognized that auditing is a practical function, and the cost of the audit must be commensurate with its value to the client. Therefore, it is essential that the audit be performed not only proficiently but with a minimum amount of time so that the client can afford the service. It is a further objective of this book to outline efficient methods and to suggest ways in which the various auditing techniques can be adequately performed in a minimum amount of time.

There are many reasons for a client to have an audit made of his financial records. These may range from the statutory, such as those required by credit unions or by the Securities and Exchange Commission, to an audit made to determine whether or not an employee has been guilty of defalcation.

However, by far the most common reason for an audit to be made of a small or medium-sized business operation is for the purpose of securing credit from banks, finance companies, and major vendors. It is in this connection that the independent accountant can be of greatest value to his client, if he is aware of the data needed by the credit grantor.

If the auditor fails to provide this information, he has failed his client. Unfortunately, in the writer's discussion with bankers and finance company officials ranging over many years, it appears that many auditors have either ignored this problem or have been unaware of it. Accordingly, one of the chief purposes of this book is to assist the auditor in providing in his audit report those statements and exhibits which will enable the credit grantor to quickly and efficiently prepare his credit analysis.

The hallmark of a professional accountant is his audit report, based in turn upon the professional conduct of his audit. It is in this area that his work becomes exposed to public view. While the smaller accounting firm may not sign its name to many published reports with wide circulation, its reports do come to the attention of that segment of the business world most likely to be influential in recommending auditors and accountants. For this reason, if for no other, substandard auditing cannot be tolerated by any accounting firm which is ambitious to progress in the business world, in the community, and in the accounting profession.

FRANK P. WALKER

ACKNOWLEDGMENT

Acknowledgment is made to the American Institute of Certified Public Accountants for permission to use excerpts from Institute publications. Also, for permission to quote passages from *Analyzing Financial Statements* published by the American Institute of Banking, section of the American Bankers Association, New York, grateful acknowledgment is made.

Contents

1. Purposes of the Audit and the Auditor's Responsibility **21**

    Purposes of the Audit • 21

        For profit organizations—21
        For nonprofit organizations—24

    The Auditor's Responsibility • 24

        Auditing standards—25
        First auditing standard—26
        Second auditing standard—26
        Third auditing standard—27
        Standards of field work—28

    Audit Program • 28

2. Preparation of the Working Papers **37**

    Technical Requirements of Working Papers • 38

        Paper size—38
        Paper stock—39
        Preprinted work sheets—39
        Covers—39
        Filing—40
        Retention—40
        Headings—40
        Indexing—41
        Timesaving possibilities—43
        Auditing symbols—44

3. Examining the System of Internal Control **45**

    Client's Representations • 51

        Inventory certificate—51
        Liability certificate—52

4. Auditing Cash **55**

Audit Program • *56*
Prior to audit date—56
Subsequent to audit date—56

Working Papers Required • *57*
Cash count—57
Comparison of recorded cash receipts and bank deposits—57
Reconcile bank accounts—58
Compare cancelled checks—60
Prove footings and trace postings—60
Verification of journal entries—60

Method of Verification • *60*
Cash in bank—60
Cancelled checks—61

Requirements of Special Situations • *61*

Financial Statement Presentation • *61*

5. Auditing Receivables **63**

Audit Program • *64*
As of audit date—64
Subsequent to audit date—64

Working Papers Required • *64*
Accounts receivable—64
Notes receivable—65
Contracts receivable—65
Receivables—other—65
Bad debts reserve (or write-off)—65

Method of Verification • *70*
Trade accounts receivable—70
Notes receivable—72

Requirements of Special Situations • *75*
Financial organizations—75
Service organizations—75
Contractors—75
Utilities—76

Financial Statement Presentation • *76*

6. Auditing Inventories **79**

Audit Program • *80*
Prior to audit date—80
As of audit date—82
Subsequent to audit date—82

Working Papers Required • *83*

  Inventory count—83
  Inventory instructions—84
  Last invoice and last receiving report—86
  In-transit items—86
  Cost, extensions, and footings—86
  Consigned inventories—86
  Inventory summary—87

Method of Verification • *87*

  Purchased material—87
  Work in process and finished goods—87
  Consigned inventory—87

Requirements of Special Situations • *89*

Financial Statement Presentation • *90*

7. Auditing Prepaid Expenses and Other Assets 93

Audit Program • *94*

  Subsequent to audit date—94

Working Papers Required • *94*

  Unexpired insurance—94
  Cash value life insurance—95
  Deposits—95
  Prepaid expenses—95
  Advances to officers—98
  Advances to employees—98
  Organization expense—98
  Goodwill—98
  Patents and trademarks—98
  Covenant not to compete—98
  Deferred research and development expenses—98
  Others—99

Method of Verification • *99*

  Unexpired insurance—99
  Cash value of life insurance—99
  Deposits—100
  Prepaid expenses—100
  Advances to officers—101
  Advances to employees—101
  Organization expense—101
  Goodwill—102
  Patents, copyrights, and trademarks—102
  Research and experimental expenses—102

Requirements of Special Situations • *103*

Financial Statement Presentation • *103*

8. Auditing Fixed Assets **105**

    Audit Program • 107
       Prior to the audit date—107
       Subsequent to audit date—107

    Working Papers Required • 108
       Permanent file—108
       Current audit file—109
       Allowance for depreciation—109
       Summary of depreciation—112

    Method of Verification • 112
       Assets—112
       Accumulated depreciation—112

    Requirements of Special Situations • 112

    Financial Statement Presentation • 115

9. Auditing Notes Payable **119**

    Audit Program • 121
       As of audit date—121
       Subsequent to audit date—121

    Working Papers Required • 121
       Permanent file—121
       Current audit file—122

    Method of Verification • 122

    Requirements of Special Situations • 128

    Financial Statement Presentation • 129

10. Auditing Trade Accounts Payable **133**

    Audit Program • 134
       Prior to the audit date—134
       As of audit date—135
       Subsequent to audit date—135

    Working Papers Required • 135
       Trade accounts payable—135

    Method of Verification • 138
       Trade accounts payable—138

    Requirements of Special Situations • 140

    Financial Statement Presentation • 141

11. Auditing Accrued Taxes and Other Expenses **143**

    Audit Program • 148
       Subsequent to audit date—148

Working Papers Required • 148
Accrued payroll taxes and withheld taxes—148
Accrued income taxes payable—148
Other accrued taxes—150
Accrued expenses—151
Contingent liabilities—151

Method of Verification • 151
Accrued payroll taxes—151
Accrued withheld taxes and other withholdings—152
Accrued income taxes—152
Accrued sales taxes—152
Property taxes—153
Excise taxes—153
Miscellaneous licenses and fees—153
Contingent liabilities—154

Requirements of Special Situations • 154
Service organizations—154
Professional organizations—154

Financial Statement Presentation • 154
Supplemental information—155
Accrued income taxes—155
Accrued taxes—other—156
Accrued expenses—156
Contingent liabilities—156

12. Auditing Capital Accounts **159**
Audit Program • 160
Subsequent to audit date—160

Working Papers Required • 161
Capital accounts—161
Capital stock accounts—161
Retained earnings—161
Other surplus accounts—162

Method of Verification • 162
Capital accounts—162
Capital stock—162
Retained earnings—163
Other surplus accounts—164

Requirements of Special Situations • 164
Capital contributions—164
Nonprofit organizations—164

Financial Statement Presentation • 165

13. Auditing Income Accounts **167**
Audit Program • 169
Subsequent to audit date—169

Working Papers Required • 170
    Dividends—170
    Interest—170
    Rents—170
    Royalties—170
    Gains and losses—170
    Other income—170

Method of Verification • 170
    Dividends—172
    Interest—173
    Rents—173
    Royalties—173
    Net gains and losses—173
    Other income—174

Requirements of Special Situations • 174

Financial Statement Presentation • 175

14. Auditing Expense Accounts **179**
    Labor—180
    Cost of sales—180
    Commissions—181
    Travel and entertainment expense—181
    Advertising—184
    Taxes—184
    Rent—185
    Bad debt expense—185
    Repairs—185
    Interest—186
    Contributions—186
    Depreciation amortization depletion—186

Audit Program • 186
    Subsequent to audit date—186

Working Papers Required • 186

Method of Verification • 189

Requirements of Special Situations • 189

Financial Statement Presentation • 189

15. The Auditor's Opinion **191**
    Scope—195
    Subsequent events—197
    Unaudited statements—198

16. The Auditor's Report **199**

     Cash on hand and in banks—203
     Trade accounts receivable—204
     Other receivables—204
     Inventories—205
     Prepaid expenses—205
     Fixed assets and accumulated depreciation—206
     Other assets—206
     Notes payable—207
     Trade accounts payable—210
     Other liabilities—210
     Income taxes payable—211
     Stockholders' equity—211
     Insurance—211

   Style Manual • *212*

Index **215**

1

Purposes of the Audit and the Auditor's Responsibility

PURPOSES OF THE AUDIT

For Profit Organizations

There are many reasons for businesses operated for profit to have an audit. If two or more interests are involved (these might be two principals, a widow of a former principal, a trust, or an estate), good management will require an audit so that all owners or stockholders may receive an independent, professional opinion as to the fairness of the financial statements. This serves to confirm the proper stewardship of the management and to satisfy the shareholders that their interests are being adequately protected.

Many states require certain types of business organizations to submit audited financial statements to the applicable authorities. These businesses usually fall into the category of those handling substantial amounts of cash and other property belonging to the general public. Examples are securities brokers and dealers, insurance companies, escrow agents, trust companies not examined by federal or state bank examiners, and similar businesses. Contractors bidding on governmental jobs such as roads, bridges, and building projects are nearly always required to be bonded, and bonding companies frequently require an audit by independent public accountants before issuing such bonds. Some states require that a contractor wishing to bid on state or local projects have a minimum net worth, substantiated by an independent audit.

21

During the course of any given year, hundreds, perhaps thousands, of small and medium-sized businesses are sold. Purchasers often require that an audit be made in order to appraise the selling price of the business properly, and to protect against unrecorded liabilities. The long-form audit report is particularly useful in such instances, because it furnishes all of the detail data necessary for a full and fair appraisal of the business.

There are several hundred thousand pension, profit-sharing, and other employee benefit plans in operation in the United States, and, numerically, the largest number are in small and medium-sized businesses. Many companies, who might otherwise not have an audit made, do so in order to insure that the benefit funds are receiving the amount of contributions from the employer required by the agreement. This serves to protect the employer from any criticism by the participants, and to insure that the participants receive the amount due.

In addition, the fund itself is often audited. The purpose is not only to determine that the financial records are complete and that proper distribution has been made of all receipts to the participants, but also to insure that all of the applicable Internal Revenue Code provisions are being complied with. The Code provisions governing pension, profit-sharing, and other employee benefit funds are very complicated, and must be strictly followed if the fund is to preserve its tax-exempt status.

An audit is frequently required from business organizations operating under a franchise. As an example, franchised automobile dealers are customarily required to have an audit by independent public accountants for submission to the manufacturer whom they represent.

One of the problems peculiar to small and medium-sized businesses is the estate tax situation created when a major stockholder dies. The business organization itself may be disrupted by the loss of a key officer or employee, but this can, to some degree, be compensated by life insurance. A different problem is faced by the executor of the estate in arriving at a valuation of the shares of the corporation. Close-held corporations ordinarily have no established market values for their stock. Under such circumstances the value of the stock, for estate tax purposes, is at the discretion of the taxing authorities, who are always very optimistic as to the worth of the stock in question. Over the years, many small and medium-sized businesses have been sold in order to provide funds to pay the federal estate tax.

Good estate planning can avoid many, if not all, of such situations. One of the first requirements of estate planning is the submission of adequate data. If the corporation in question has been audited for a number of years, such data is readily available from the audit reports. A "buy-sell" agreement is often made a part of estate planning. Such an agreement can be an important factor in establishing the value of the shares for estate tax purposes. An audit is frequently required to establish the price of the stock in the event that one shareholder wishes to sell, or in the event of the death of one of the owners.

In the case of businesses operated for profit, however, by far the most common reason for the audit of small and medium-sized firms, whose stock is not listed on an exchange or is not actively traded over the counter, is for the purpose of securing credit.

This credit may be from banks, finance companies, or, in some cases, from major vendors.

There is a secondary advantage of an audit accruing to the client, which ultimately may prove to be more valuable to him than the audit report itself. This is the advice and counsel that the auditor may supply his client as a result of making the audit. One benefit, arising from the examination of the client's system of internal control, is the auditor's recommendations for tightening the handling of cash, inventory, and other assets of the organization. In some instances, an audit may disclose that the client's financial position is much better than he or his creditors believed, so that the client may be entitled to more favorable credit terms. Improving efficiency of office management and the handling of paper work falls within the scope of the auditor's professional competence, and he can often suggest methods for reducing costs in this area.

It is surprising how often the auditor will discover that his client actually does not receive the periodic financial information from his accounting records that are of utmost importance in the making of day-to-day business decisions. Accordingly, the auditor is in an excellent position to recommend methods of furnishing this information in a practical form. In subsequent chapters, treating the various subjects of the audit, suggestions will be made as to how the auditor can help his client in these areas.

While the audit procedures outlined in the following chapters will apply to all audits, they are designed particularly for audits of profit-making organizations: proprietorships, partnerships, and corporations.

In addition to meeting the auditor's responsibilities, which are discussed in detail in subsequent portions of this chapter, it is necessary that the auditor prepare his report in such a manner as to furnish the information which will enable the credit grantor to evaluate the financial responsibility of the client. Failure to provide this information may prevent the client from getting deserved credit, which may be essential for his continuing operation, and may lose a customer for the prospective credit grantor. The auditor, therefore, must be cognizant of the information which the credit grantor requires.

In *Analyzing Financial Statements* [1] the authors state:

> Each businessman must know whether his business is operating at a profit or loss. The financial condition of the business at all times must be known to its management.

This is the specific information that an audit will disclose. The value of the audit lies in the independent professional opinion expressed by the auditor. The classic approach to granting credit is expressed as "Character, Capacity, and Capital." The independent accountant cannot express an opinion as to character, but his report can be analyzed to determine capacity and capital.

It should be recognized that a credit grantor can make a credit analysis of a prospective customer only if he has data available for analysis. In the absence of a

---

[1] Carlisle R. Davis and Edward F. Gee, *Analyzing Financial Statements,* American Institute of Banking, New York, N. Y.

report by an independent accountant, he must depend upon data furnished by the prospective customer, which often is incomplete, and in addition is impossible to assess for validity. Accordingly, most credit grantors prefer to work from an audit report, prepared by a competent, independent public accountant.

Regarding the source of data of an applicant for credit, *Analyzing Financial Statements,* (op cit) has this to say:

> The examination and certification of financial statements by independent Certified Public Accountants is perhaps the best available assurance of the reliability of the figures.

An important part of this manual will be the suggestions of data to be included in the report which is essential for the credit analysis of the client's financial position. In addition, the cost of the audit must be limited to an amount that can be economically justified, so that throughout this manual suggestions will be made as to the most efficient ways in which the auditing procedures can be carried out.

Nonprofit Organizations

There are many reasons for an organization to have an audit made of its financial records. In the case of governmental agencies, such an audit may be required by statute. In the case of nonprofit organizations, such as community funds, hospitals, and other public, charitable, and educational organizations it may be a matter of policy.

Among such agencies which customarily require an audit by an independent public accountant are the following:

1. Federal and state credit unions.
2. School boards.
3. Municipal agencies such as water and utility departments.
4. Colleges and universities.
5. Federal governmental grants.
6. Labor unions.
7. Certain trusts and estates.

Before starting an audit which involves any governmental agency, or any organization supervised by a governmental agency, the auditor should familiarize himself with any peculiarities of the audit which may be required by statute. In many cases these are quite detailed, while in others they require only the usual independent auditor's examination. In a book of this size, it is not practicable to detail the statutory requirements of such agencies, particularly since they will vary greatly from one state to another, and in addition they are subject to frequent change.

THE AUDITOR'S RESPONSIBILITY

The auditor, under present conditions, accepts a rather awesome responsibility when he undertakes an audit. It is well established that the financial statements are those of management. The function of the independent public accountant, in making an audit of the financial statements, is to express his professional opinion as to the fairness, the consistency, and the compliance with generally accepted accounting principles of those statements. This is all that he undertakes to do. He cannot insure nor can he guaranty the statements.

> The fact that a financial statement has been audited by a reputable firm of independent Certified Public Accountants is no guaranty against dishonesty. The public accountant is not a detective, and when there is nothing to arouse his suspicions, it is not incumbent upon him to expect fraud or to conduct an examination of the type that might lead to the disclosure of fraud. Therefore, the normal scope of an examination for bank credit purposes cannot be relied upon conclusively to disclose the existence of fraudulent practices on the part of business management.[2]

That the financial statements are those of the client, and that the auditor is only expressing his professional opinion thereon is well understood by the accounting profession, but unfortunately this premise is not universally accepted, in spite of the effort of bankers, as quoted above, to educate readers as to the real meaning of the audited statement.

This tendency, on the part of some readers of the financial statements, to read more into the auditor's opinion than is intended has led to misunderstandings and lawsuits. The liability of the auditor to third parties in the United States was originally determined in *Ultramares*[3] and was generally followed by the courts until fairly recent times. Lately, however, there has been a tendency to extend the auditor's legal liability.

Auditing Standards

To protect himself, the auditor is primarily dependent upon his strict observance of all of the auditing standards as set forth by competent authority.

These are standards which have been developed over the years by the accounting profession and have been adopted in general by the Securities and Exchange Commission, which is responsible for establishing the reporting standards of corporations coming under its jurisdiction. While most small and medium-sized businesses do not fall under the supervision or jurisdiction of the Securities and Exchange Commission, the auditor of the smaller companies is bound by the same standards as those required for auditing the very largest organizations.

Auditing standards, in general, comprise the following:

1. General standards.
2. Standards of field work.
3. Standards of reporting.

---

[2] Carlisle R. Davis and Edward F. Gee, *Analyzing Financial Statements,* American Institute of Banking, New York, N. Y.

[3] *Ultramares,* New York Court of Appeals, 1931.

Failure to comply with all of the applicable standards may render the auditor liable for civil penalties, and as has been shown by at least one court decision, for criminal fraud. Thus, before he starts his audit, the auditor is on notice that he is bound to conform to generally accepted auditing standards.

Successful auditing rests squarely upon two principles: the application of the appropriate auditing procedures and the observation of applicable auditing standards. Simply stated, procedures are the acts to be performed, while standards represent the measure of the quality of the work done. This book is concerned primarily with auditing procedures, and although it is assumed that the reader is familiar with auditing standards, reference will be made, from time to time, to the applicable auditing standards.

The general auditing standards are as follows: [4]

1. The examination is to be performed by a person or persons having adequate technical training and proficiency as an auditor.
2. In all matters relating to the assignment, an independence in mental attitude is to be maintained by the auditor or auditors.
3. Due professional care is to be exercised in the performance of the examination and the preparation of the report.

First Auditing Standard

To meet the requirements of paragraph number one in the preceding list, the auditor will necessarily have completed his formal training and will have had the actual auditing experience requisite to the performance of a level of proficiency appropriate to the audit. Experience is gained only by doing. Normally the auditor will have worked for a period of time under competent supervision, and he will endeavor to improve his experience by constant review of his work, by study, and particularly by keeping abreast of developments in auditing principles and procedures. He will be equally alert to the development of accounting principles.

Second Auditing Standard

In the matter of independence, the auditor must be independent not only in fact but in mental attitude. This means that he is without bias with respect to his client, either favorably or unfavorably; that he has the attitude of an impartial observer, so that he may report upon the results of operations and upon financial statements of the client in complete fairness to its management, its stockholders, and its creditors.

Obviously, the auditor can hold no position with his client in which management decisions are made. Likewise he can have no financial interest, either directly or indirectly, in the company being audited, or in any company or organization having material dealings with the client. This requirement applies equally to each member of his auditing staff and other employees. The prudent auditor will maintain a record of

---

[4] "Auditing Standards and Procedures," Statement on Auditing Procedure No. 33, AICPA, New York, N. Y.

financial investments of himself, each partner, and each employee, to make certain that full compliance with this canon of auditing is met. Obviously, any personal or family relationship between any partner or employee of the auditor and persons in a management capacity with the client must be carefully scrutinized, and the auditor must satisfy himself that such relationships are not sufficiently close as to preclude the proper degree of independence. It is in the area of independence that the auditor has been most subject to criticism from the press, from stockholders, from security analysts, and others. In this respect, the question of the auditor's supplying management services has been the subject of a great deal of discussion and some controversy, not only within the profession, but among businessmen generally. It is argued that in providing management services, the independent accountant is not making management decisions but is recommending to his clients methods and procedures for the efficient gathering and analysis of the data. Because of his wide experience and training in this area and familiarity with his clients' problems, the independent accountant is in a unique position to serve his client.

On the other hand, it is suggested that the independent accountant is invariably influenced, to some degree, by the fact that having made recommendations to management he may be inclined to view results in a somewhat more favorable light. At the present time, the professional code of ethics places no restriction upon the furnishing of management services. To avoid criticism, it is desirable that the partner or staff member furnishing management services have no connection with the audit of that particular client. However, such division of responsibility is not always possible with smaller accounting offices.

Third Auditing Standard

Probably the greatest test of an auditor's professional qualifications falls in the the area of determining what auditing procedures are necessary, in the circumstances of a particular audit, to justify his professional opinion. It is the responsibility of the independent auditor, having full knowledge of the applicable auditing standards, to determine to what extent and by what methods he will conduct his examination. In this connection, it is appropriate to refer the auditor to the "Opinions of the Accounting Principles Board" of the American Institute of Certified Public Accountants,[5] as representing the prevailing opinions of the accounting profession, with which the auditor is presumed not only to be familiar but by which he is bound in expressing his opinion of the client's financial statements.

The following chapters present in detail the subjects most often encountered in the audit of small and medium-sized organizations. Space limitations will not permit covering registration and reporting for the Securities and Exchange Commission, the handling of foreign subsidiaries, reporting large mergers, and similar situations usually encountered only in large business organizations.

Small and medium-sized companies are found in every segment of American

---

[5] "Opinions of the Accounting Principles Board," AICPA, New York, N. Y.

business, manufacturing, wholesale, retail, and service industries, and the professions. Each geographical section of the country has its local specialties. For example, in the oil-producing areas of the United States the auditor can expect to be called upon to audit oil and gas exploration and development enterprises; near the seacoast he may be expected to audit fishing, towing, and stevedoring businesses.

While the auditing of all financial records requires exactly the same basic procedures and calls for the application of the same basic auditing standards, each business has its own peculiarities. Preliminary study by the auditor, before starting the audit of a member of an industry which he has not previously audited, can be highly profitable. It will give the auditor familiarity with the peculiar vocabulary of the industry, and give him some advance knowledge of specific situations requiring special attention. Practically every type of business enterprise in the United States has a trade association. Often these trade associations publish accounting and bookkeeping manuals, with suggested standard account classification. When these are available, the auditor should secure and study them before starting the first audit. Even if the client does not use such standardized material, the knowledge of them may often save the auditor much time on a first audit.

In addition to publications of trade associations, there are, of course, many published books and manuals on accounting and bookkeeping for specific industries and trades. Many of these are worthwhile subjects of study for the auditor who is preparing to audit an industry member for the first time.

Standards of Field Work

The second of the general auditing standards, standards of field work, are as follows: [6]

1. The work is to be adequately planned and assistants, if any, are to be properly supervised.
2. There is a proper study and evaluation of the existing internal control as a basis for reliance thereon, and for the determination of the resultant extent of the tests to which auditing procedures are to be restricted.
3. Sufficient competent evidential matter is to be obtained through inspection, observation, inquiries, and confirmations to afford a reasonable basis for an opinion regarding the financial statements under examination.

AUDIT PROGRAM

The first standard of field work states that "The field work is to be adequately planned . . . ." This can best be accomplished by the use of the "Audit Program." This is a written plan or outline of the various procedures to be followed in performing the audit. While the exact form is unimportant, most firms find it convenient and

---

[6] "Auditing Standards and Procedures," Statements on Auditing Procedure No. 33, AICPA, New York.

efficient to use a printed outline which will fit the working papers and which will provide such information as when and by whom the work was performed, time required, and by whom the work was reviewed. It often serves as an index for the working papers. A number of printed standard forms are available for this purpose, although most accounting firms prefer to develop their own.

One of the most useful functions of the audit program is to insure that no essential audit procedure is omitted. It must be emphasized, however, that no two clients and no two audits are exactly alike. A slavish following of a predetermined program may result in failure to follow up data which may be disclosed by preliminary review. The competent auditor will use the program as an outline, which forms a useful starting point, but applies his knowledge and experience to insure that no phase is slighted or omitted.

Following is a basic outline, which in no sense is to be considered a complete program, but which may be useful in the development of the audit program.

AUDIT PROGRAM

(Each item must be completed. If not applicable indicate by N/A. Program must be approved by partner in charge before work is started.)

Client:

Address:

Official to contact: *Title:*

Audit date: *Auditor in charge:*

Partner in charge:

Type of organization:

	Auditor	Date completed	Reviewed by
General:			
1. Confirm in good standing, state of _____	_____	_____	_____
2. Review minutes	_____	_____	_____
3. Prepare internal control questionnaire	_____	_____	_____
4. List additional procedures indicated by #3	_____	_____	_____

Figure 1-1

	Auditor	*Date completed*	*Review-ed by*
Cash:			
5. Confirm and reconcile all bank balances at audit date	_____	_____	_____
6. Confirm and reconcile cut-off date balances	_____	_____	_____
7. Count cash, notes receivable, and other securities	_____	_____	_____
8. Verify cutoff cash receipts	_____	_____	_____
9. Compare cancelled checks (List bank accounts and number of months for each)	_____	_____	_____
10. Compare recorded cash receipts and bank statements	_____	_____	_____
11. Test journal footings and general ledger postings	_____	_____	_____
12. Test detail of cash receipts and detail of bank deposit slips for evidence of lapping	_____	_____	_____
13. Special cash procedures (list)	_____	_____	_____
Receivables:			
14. Confirm receivables	_____	_____	_____
15. Verify cutoff of shipping and billing	_____	_____	_____
16. Review bad debt write-offs, recoveries, and adequacy of bad debt allowances	_____	_____	_____
17. Special receivable procedures (list)	_____	_____	_____
Inventories:			
18. Review inventory instructions and amend if necessary	_____	_____	_____

Figure 1-1 (contd.)

	Auditor	Date completed	Reviewed by
19. Observe inventory count	_____	_____	_____
20. Verify listing, pricing, extension, and footing of inventory	_____	_____	_____
21. Secure Inventory Certificate	_____	_____	_____
22. Special inventory procedures (list)	_____	_____	_____

Fixed assets:

23. Verify additions to and retirements of fixed assets	_____	_____	_____
24. Review provision for depreciation for year, and reconcile allowance for depreciation accounts	_____	_____	_____
25. Special fixed asset procedures (list)	_____	_____	_____

Other assets:

26. Review and confirm all other assets	_____	_____	_____
27. Special procedures for other assets (list)	_____	_____	_____

Liabilities:

28. Verify cutoff of receiving	_____	_____	_____
29. Verify that all material received had been reflected in payables	_____	_____	_____
30. Confirm accounts payable	_____	_____	_____
31. Confirm all notes, contracts, and other written instruments payable	_____	_____	_____
32. Review all tax returns and tax accruals	_____	_____	_____

Figure 1-1 (contd.)

	Auditor	*Date completed*	*Review-ed by*
33. Review accrued payroll	_____	_____	_____
34. Review all other accrued liabilities	_____	_____	_____
35. Request letters from all attorneys serving client regarding pending litigation and unpaid fees	_____	_____	_____
36. Inspect state and/or county recorders' records for unrecorded liabilities	_____	_____	_____
37. Secure Liability Certificate	_____	_____	_____
38. Prepare income tax returns	_____	_____	_____

Income accounts:

39. Review all income accounts	_____	_____	_____
40. Analyze selected accounts (list)	_____	_____	_____
41. Verify as required	_____	_____	_____

Expense accounts:

42. Review all expense accounts	_____	_____	_____
43. Analyze selected accounts	_____	_____	_____
44. Verify as required	_____	_____	_____

Capital accounts:

45. Verify capital stock issued and outstanding	_____	_____	_____
46. Analyze retained earnings account	_____	_____	_____
47. Analyze any other capital accounts	_____	_____	_____
48. Analyze partners' capital and drawing accounts	_____	_____	_____
49. Analyze proprietor's capital and drawing accounts	_____	_____	_____

Figure 1-1 (contd.)

As a supplement, a master time schedule should be prepared. Certain procedures, for example checking the cutoff of invoices and receiving reports, must be done on a certain date, and a time schedule will prevent such procedures from being overlooked. Subject chapters will indicate for each element of the audit the preferred time at which it should be done, which should be incorporated in the master time schedule. Following is one form of a master time schedule.

MASTER TIME SCHEDULE

(This schedule must be prepared for each audit prior to the start of the field work, and be approved by the partner in charge of the audit.)

Client:

Audit date (balance sheet date):

Auditor in charge:

Partner in charge:

As of audit date:

	Date required	Completed
Cash count	_____	_____
Security count	_____	_____
Verify cutoff of cash receipts	_____	_____
Special cash procedures (list)	_____	_____
Verify cutoff of shipping	_____	_____
Verify cutoff of receiving	_____	_____
Observe inventory count	_____	_____
Other special procedures (list)	_____	_____

Prior to audit date:

Assignment letter (if required)	_____	_____
Prepare audit program	_____	_____
Arrange with client for accounts receivable confirmation requests	_____	_____
Review and approve client's instructions for physical count of inventory	_____	_____
Prepare internal control questionnaire	_____	_____

Figure 1-2

	Date required	Completed
Prepare bank confirmation requests	_____	_____
Prepare accounts and notes payable confirmation requests	_____	_____
Prepare requests for confirmation from attorneys, governmental agencies, etc. (list)	_____	_____
Review minutes of meetings of directors and stockholders	_____	_____
Schedule all other preliminary work which can be performed prior to audit work (list)	_____	_____

Subsequent to audit date:

Prepare detail list in accordance with audit program	_____	_____

Figure 1-2 (contd.)

The audit program starts with a discussion with the client to establish the primary purpose of the audit. While the purpose of the audit does not in any way change the basic auditing principles and procedures to be followed, it does point to certain phases which may require additional attention. In discussing a proposed audit with the client, the auditor should take great care to explain exactly what the purpose and the results will be. The officers of many small and medium-sized corporations often have not had training or experience in financial matters and do not have the financial sophistication to understand that an audit is made primarily for the purpose of expressing an accountant's opinion and will not necessarily expose fraud or other irregularities, should such actually exist. Even though an audit is being made at the request or suggestion of a bank or other credit grantor, if it is a first audit, the client must be made aware of exactly what the audit is and is not.

There is some divergence of opinion among auditors as to the value of an assignment letter and what should be included therein. Obviously, it is of more importance in the case of a new client than with clients for whom work has been performed over a period of years. In the latter case, letters are frequently omitted unless there is some basic change to be made.

Generally, however, there is a great deal to be said for having such a letter in the auditor's file should any dispute or question arise in the future. Certainly if there is to be any restriction of auditing procedures they must be spelled out in the assignment letter in complete detail. It is well to note also, that regardless of what may be contained in any correspondence with the client, the auditor's responsibility for his work and his opinion is in no way changed. If there is any question in the mind of the auditor as to his ability to conduct a proper audit under restrictions imposed by the client he should refuse the assignment, since such restrictions do not constitute a defense for an inadequate audit or an improper opinion.

There is no particular form for a letter of assignment. It may simply describe briefly the proposed work to be done, the balance sheet date, and the period covered by the income account. Such a letter would be normal for audits which have been regularly performed over a period of years. Or it may be quite elaborate, depending upon the circumstances. In the case of a first audit, it will usually be quite detailed, containing, for example, the type of work to be done, what the report is to include, whether or not there are to be any limitations on the opinion, and the extent to which the client's staff is to assist. It is also good practice to indicate when the books are to be ready for the auditor.

The following letter is one used by the writer. The letter is ordinarily addressed to the company, to the attention of the officer responsible for the engagement:

Board of Directors
XYZ Corporation
Our Town, State
Gentlemen:

Atten: Mr. John Doe, Chairman, Board of Directors

Confirming our discussion of July 10, 19xx, we will make an examination and a report thereon of the books and records of the XYZ Corporation as of September 30, 19xx, and for the 12 months then ending, in accordance with generally accepted auditing procedures. It is understood that your staff will assist us to the extent practicable, including the preparation of your customers' monthly statements for the purpose of requesting confirmation of the amounts due you, and preparation of requests for confirmation of notes and accounts payable.

We understand that your employees will make a physical count of the inventory, starting September 29, 19xx, at which time our representatives will be present to observe and make tests of the count; and we further understand that you expect to have the books and records available for our examination on or about October 15, 19xx.

It is understood that this examination is made primarily for the purpose of expressing our opinion on the financial statements of the Corporation, and will not necessarily disclose irregularities (should any exist).

Our report will include a short form report, comprising our opinion on the Balance Sheet and Statement of Retained Earnings as of September 30, 19xx, and Statement of Income and Source and Application of Funds for the year then ended. In addition we will furnish supplemental financial information, which while not audited, will be obtained from the accounting records tested by us as part of the auditing procedures to be followed by us in our examination of the above financial statements.

> Our fee for this service will be based upon the time required, in accordance with the schedule furnished you.
>
>   Very truly yours,
>
>   A B C, CPAs

If the audit report is to be of maximum value to the client and to his bank or other credit grantor, it is essential that it contain sufficient information to supply all of the data which will be required to make a proper evaluation of the credit situation. For this reason, in each of the following chapters, beginning with Chapter 4, one section is devoted to "Financial Statement Presentation." The purpose of this is not only to review the various ways in which an item may be presented on one of the four major financial statements—Balance Sheet, Income Account, Analysis of Retained Earnings, and Statement of Source and Application of Funds—but also to supply the supplementary information needed.

The accountant should remember that he is being judged on the quality of his work by all who read and examine or otherwise make use of his report. With regard to the use of the report in granting credit, the authors of *Analyzing Financial Statements* say:

> The appraisal of the accountants who certified to the statements of a business is an important part of the appraisal of a credit risk. The accountants should be unquestionably honest and independent, fully experienced in examining businesses of the type under consideration, and well-qualified by training and intelligence to do a competent job.

From the foregoing it is readily apparent that the loan officer of the bank or the finance company is going to consider not only the factual material in the report but the qualifications and reputation of the auditor himself.

2

Preparation of the Working Papers

The third standard of field work reads:

> Sufficient, competent, evidential matter is to be obtained through inspection, inquiries, and confirmations to afford a reasonable basis for an opinion regarding the financial statements under examination.[1]

Subsequent chapters treat in detail the working papers required for each of the various areas of the audit. However, it should always be remembered that no one volume can contain all of the possible variations of working papers which may be required for specific audits. Therefore, it should be noted that while these are useful as a basis for the audit, they are not intended to be definitive.

Working papers must be complete, and must be prepared in such a manner that they will be comprehensible a week, a month, or ten years later. The safest precept to follow is to assume that every working paper prepared may become evidence in a court case.

While the working papers provide the "evidential matter," as set forth in the third standard of field work, they also constitute evidence of proper planning and the extent to which the various audit procedures have been carried out. In addition, by receiving the proper review, they show that the necessary supervision, which is demanded by the first standard of field work, has been adequately effected.

The audit papers are the property of the auditor and some states have given

---

[1] "Auditing Standards and Procedures," American Institute of Certified Public Accountants, New York.

recognition to this by statute. The working papers are, of course, to be considered completely confidential, and in accordance with the canons of professional ethics none of the material appearing therein may be disclosed to any unauthorized person. It would appear, however, that the auditor's work papers are not considered as privileged matter by the federal courts in income tax cases, and are subject to subpoena in such instances. This is frequently the situation in state courts when the point at issue is criminal rather than civil. The auditor should get the opinion of his own legal counsel as it applies to his own state.

In examining the financial records of small and medium-sized businesses, the auditor will often find that the client's records are not complete. Accordingly, he will, in his working papers, in effect complete the necessary records. It should be kept in mind, however, that these papers remain the property of the auditor and should not be considered in any way as a part of the client's financial records.

One of the faults often found in smaller accounting organizations is lack of attention to the preparation of audit working papers, particularly by junior accountants. In even the smallest organizations, a definite procedure should be established and followed for the review of the work papers of an audit. This gives an additional incentive to the field auditor to prepare adequate working papers.

Since preparing the working papers is an important part of every audit, it is well to provide a permanent guide to their proper preparation. Even the smallest auditing firm, including individual practitioners, can prepare a working manual on the acceptable method of preparing working papers. This might include the following:

1. Size and kind of work paper forms to be used.

   Note: *This might include printed and letter forms such as bank confirmations, accounts receivable confirmation requests, etc.*

2. Covers to be used.
3. Filing instructions.
4. Headings to be used.
5. Indexing.
6. Symbols to be used.
7. Review instructions.

This information can be treated as a separate manual or included in a general auditing manual.

TECHNICAL REQUIREMENTS OF WORKING PAPERS

Paper Size

The paper used is primarily one of personal preference. The traditional accountants' work sheets are 8 1/2″ by 14″, top bound—which is standard "legal" size, with double or triple folds as required to provide for a greater number of columns. These have the obvious advantage of permitting a large number of horizontal lines (usually 45 to 50) on each sheet. The disadvantage of the legal size is in the filing, plus the fact that they are somewhat more clumsy to use. In recent years, there has been a trend on the part of a number of accounting firms to use 8 1/2″ by 11″ sheets bound on the side. This permits filing in standard letter-size file cabinets. In order to keep inventories of paper at a minimum, most firms standardize on three or four sizes and styles of work sheets. The most common of these are two or four column with name space, 8 1/2″ width, and 12 or 14 column, 17″ width for work sheets requiring more vertical columns. Occasionally, a three fold with 18 or 21 vertical columns is used, but unless the work area is rather extensive these become extremely difficult to work with and should be avoided if possible.

Paper Stock

Oddly enough, except for the change from white work paper, which produced a rather disagreeable glare, to buff or green paper, which is easier on the eyes, there has been very little change in paper stock. Almost the only discernible difference in work sheets is the box, or lack of it, printed at the top right-hand corner for date and auditor's initials. On most paper, the horizontal lines are numbered and the columns are numbered—a useful, though not essential, feature.

Preprinted Work Sheets

Over the years there have been numerous experiments using preprinted forms of working papers. In certain cases, these appear to have a considerable advantage. For example, if an audit is being conducted on a retail establishment where there are eight or ten or more cash registers or cashiers' funds which must be counted, it would appear that a standard printed form listing the various denominations of coins and bills, together with a printed receipt form, would save the auditor's time. Likewise, where sheets which require numerous columnar headings (such as the work paper for computing unexpired insurance premiums) are involved, a great deal of time could be saved by the use of such forms. However, the disadvantage is that the field auditor must carry quite a variety of forms, and for this reason, perhaps, preprinted forms have not gained as much general usage as might be expected. In the future, as labor costs continue to increase, it is quite likely that they will be favored.

Covers

An infinite variety of covers are available, and the choice is one of personal preference. The cost of imprinting the accountant's name on the work paper covers is very small, and will add to his status when observed by clients. One additional advantage of using a standard 8 1/2″ by 11″ side-bind sheet is that it will fit a standard three-ring binder which is convenient for field use prior to the completion of the audit. If two or more men are working on the audit at one time, several such binders can conveniently be used, each containing one audit section.

Filing

While filing cabinets are still most commonly used for storage, the new type of horizontal racks, which are available with doors and locks, will permit the filing of approximately three times as much per square foot of space occupied as the conventional four- or five-drawer file. They have the additional advantage that two or more people can remove or replace files at one time.

Retention

Another question that arises is how long audit working papers should be retained. The best available answer seems to be "forever." Almost no authority is willing to put a specific limit on the time that files should be kept and the general practice is to keep them indefinitely. Obviously, after three or four years—and three years seems to be the average—they can be transferred from "active," where they must be easily available, to "inactive" which might be in a public warehouse, if office space is inadequate. Some public storage firms make a specialty of providing secure fireproof space for office records.

Microfilming is beginning to be used extensively for working papers and often it is no more costly than safe storage. Microfilm has the additional advantage of fitting in a bank safety deposit box if so desired.

Headings

Audit working papers should have as the minimum the following headings:

1. Name of client.

   Note: *It often saves time to put the client's name on the papers with a rubber stamp at the conclusion of the audit. However, if working papers are not kept carefully segregated, it is always possible for them to become intermingled with those of another client. One suggestion is to stamp up one or two pads of working paper prior to starting the audit.*

2. Date of preparation.

   Note: *This assumes great importance in the event that material is subsequently discovered which may change the results of earlier auditing procedures. In such an event it is absolutely imperative that the date at which the various work papers were prepared is in evidence. In subsequent chapters, under the subject of "working papers," it will be suggested that working papers from prior years be brought forward. In this instance, the date of the later audit would be put directly under the earlier date, and the initials of the auditor of the later audit would be placed under those of the auditor performing the prior work. For example:*

$$10\text{-}6\text{-}19xw \quad JWD \quad FSW$$
$$11\text{-}1\text{-}19xx \quad LMS \quad FSW$$

In the example above, the first set of initials would be those of the auditor, the second set those of the partner or supervisor reviewing the work.

3. Initials (or name) of the auditor preparing the work sheet.

4. Initials (or name) of the person reviewing the work sheet.

5. Subject.

   Note: *Usually it is advisable to put no more than one subject on a work sheet. An exception might be if there are a number of accounts to be analyzed, each consisting of only one or two entries; in such case it would be satisfactory to include several on one work sheet.*

6. Balance sheet date and/or period covered by the audit.

Indexing

For efficient review and later reference, working papers must be indexed. One of the oldest methods, and one still often encountered, is the one of simply taking a colored pencil and, starting with the first page after the papers have been bound, numbering it "1," the next "2," and going through the entire file, assigning a sequential number to each. After this has been done, an index sheet is prepared, starting with the first item and continuing through the file. In this case, the working papers are usually filed in working trial balance order, with such items as minutes, internal control questionnaire, and other nonworking trial balance items at the front of the file.

The disadvantage of this system is that the indexing is usually done after the working papers and the audit report have been reviewed, and the reviewers have to work through the papers without an index.

Another method, used by many firms, is to have a standardized index, which is usually printed, so that a copy of the index can be placed at the beginning of each set of working papers. This is usually based upon normal trial balance order and might be set up as follows:

A. *Cash:*

1. Cash count.

2. Bank reconciliation—audit date.

3. Bank reconciliation—cutoff date.

4. Comparison of recorded cash receipts with bank statements.

5. Check comparisons.

6. Footings.

7. Depository verification.

etc.

   Note: *In using an index of this type, the pages would be numbered in accordance with the index. For example, the petty cash count would be "A-1-1," the* *letter "A" indicating cash, the first "1" indicating cash count, and the final "1" indicating that it comprised one sheet. If there were several cash funds the second, third, and fourth cash funds would be designated A-1-2, A-1-3, A-1-4, etc.*

The disadvantage of a system such as this is that in order to cover all contingencies, the index has to be rather complex. To illustrate, many accounts found in auditing a school board do not appear in auditing a radio station. Likewise, many accounts found in a manufacturing concern will not appear in a mercantile business. The advantage of such a system is that the partner or supervisor reviewing the audit will have pretty well memorized the basic index and, therefore, to some extent at least, it will save his time in reviewing the work.

A somewhat more flexible system is to use the working trial balance as the basis for the index. In this system, one variation would assign capital letters of the alphabet to the assets, lower case letters to the liabilities. If the number of accounts are more than 26, double letters are used. Income accounts would be designated with double letters, the first capital, the second lower case, and expense accounts with double letters, the first lower case and the second capital.

After the trial balance has been prepared from the general ledger, which usually is one of the first steps in the audit, a colored pencil is used to indicate the indexing (conveniently at the extreme left or at the extreme right). Following is an illustration:

ASSETS

Imprest cash fund	AA
Cash in Blank National Bank	AB-1
Cash in Fourth National Bank	AB-2
Cash in General Trust Co.	AB-3
Accounts receivable	AC-1-15

> **Note:** *The "1-15" indicates that the accounts receivable trial balance contains 15 pages of work sheets.*

LIABILITIES

Notes payable—bank secured	aa
Notes payable—other	ab
Accounts payable	ac-1-6

> **Note:** *The "1-6" indicates that accounts payable trial balance contains six pages of work sheets.*

INCOME ACCOUNTS

Sales—Department A	Aa-1
Sales—Department B	Aa-2
Sales—Department C	Aa-3
Cash discount earned	Ab

EXPENSE ACCOUNTS

Cost of sales—Department A	aA-1
Cost of sales—Department B	aA-2
Cost of sales—Department C	aA-3
Commissions	aB

etc.

If additional accounts are added during the course of the audit, which is often the case, a subnumber can be used as a suffix. For example, in the above illustration, if a fourth bank account were discovered, it could be designated as "AB-4." Where there are several sheets in a category, as in the accounts receivable trial balance, they would be numbered consecutively in the order in which they are prepared.

While such a system lacks the uniformity which is characteristic of the standardized system, it has the advantage of being easily applied, and does not require the use of an additional index sheet, since the working trial balance itself becomes the index. Non-trial-balance subjects, such as minutes, internal control questionnaire, etc. are usually placed at the beginning of the file and indexed separately.

Whatever system of indexing is adopted should be made uniform for the entire auditing staff. The most practical way to do this is to describe in detail the method to be used and put it in a manual. In this manner, all staff members will be informed as to the correct procedure for indexing audit working papers.

Timesaving Possibilities

Two areas which seem to offer considerable possibilities for saving an auditor time are the use of copying machines and the use of dictating equipment. Virtually every client has a copying machine of some sort. In many cases, as will be pointed out in subsequent chapters, it is much quicker to make a copy of minutes, invoices, cancelled checks, agreements, and other documents, than it is to abstract them. In addition to the time saved, the reviewer has access to a copy of the actual document in question and is not dependent upon an abstract in which an essential part might have been omitted. The author has found that in some cases it has been practicable to photocopy a journal page rather than copy it by hand. Sometimes this single item alone can save an hour or more. In any event the auditor should be alert for any possible time savings, as well as improving the quality of his working papers by photocopying material. The client is usually more than happy to stand the small expense of such copies, compared to the cost of the auditor's time which would otherwise be required. In the case of clients who do not possess a satisfactory copying machine, and if there is sufficient material involved, it may be advisable to rent or borrow a copier.

While most auditing firms have been making at least a minimum use of copying methods, a second field appears to the writer to offer extensive savings in the cost of field work, and has been largely ignored by the accounting profession. This is the use of dictating equipment. Modern technology has produced recorders of various types which are portable and very dependable. Rather than have the auditor laboriously write out in longhand (and for auditors, like physicians, poor handwriting seems a necessary requirement for entering the profession), it would be better to have him dictate his findings and have them transcribed in his office. Stenographic time is usually less costly than the auditor's time. The writer has noticed also that many of the reports are still being written by hand by the field auditor or supervisor when these could easily be dictated, at a great saving in time.

Good dictating, like any other professional skill, requires some training and experience. Not everyone is a naturally competent dictator. However, this is a skill which is readily learned and presents no particular problems.

Another area in which a recording device could certainly be used is in the physical checking of the inventory count. As will be pointed out in Chapter 6, some professional organizations use recorders, which are portable and employ a neck microphone. Rather than making actual notations on work paper, the man making the inventory count simply talks into the microphone. With the development of suitable equipment, and proper training in its use, this method can be just as accurate, and the auditor can cover many more items by using such a check than if he were to write down each item checked. In most instances, it would be necessary to have the tape recordings transcribed, but again, stenographic time is less costly than auditing time.

Auditing Symbols

All auditors use written symbols to indicate action taken with regard to audit figures. While the custom is universal, the meaning of the specific symbols varies with each office or firm (probably inherited from the most senior partner). Auditor's "tick" marks are countless years old, probably dating from the earliest double-entry set of books. Other symbols frequently used are:

V   to indicate that the item has been verified, as by tracing to an invoice or other original document.

C   to indicate compared, as comparing the entry in the cash disbursements book with a cancelled check.

✓/ to indicate that a column of figures has been proved.

∕∕ to indicate that the posting has been traced to a book of original entry.

The exact symbols used are not significant, but it is important that an accounting office restrict its writing to an approved list of symbols, so that all members of the auditing staff will be speaking the same language. This is a good subject to include in the manual for working papers or the auditing manual.

3

Examining the System
of Internal Control

The second standard of field work states:

There is to be a proper study and evaluation of the existing internal control as the basis for reliance thereon and for the determination of the resultant extent of the tests to which auditing procedures are to be restricted.[1]

Internal control is defined in this manner:

Internal control comprises the plan of organization and all of the coordinate methods and measures adopted within a business to safeguard its assets, check the accuracy and reliability of its accounting data, promote operational efficiency, and encourage adherence to prescribed managerial policies.[1]

This definition represents an ideal which, unfortunately, is seldom encountered in auditing small and medium-sized businesses. A large business organization ordinarily has developed rather detailed and elaborate accounting manuals. These serve not only as a statement of policy but as specific instructions in the execution of that policy. In addition, most companies of this size have a staff of internal auditors, or at least a department which undertakes this function, reporting directly to a senior officer. The internal auditing staff can, therefore, insure not only that the detailed accounting procedures are properly followed but also that company policy is followed.

In small business organizations, with the possible exception of professional groups, emphasis is placed upon sales, for the reason that no business can exist or

---

[1] "Statements on Auditing Procedure No. 33," Committee on Auditing Procedure of the American Institute of Certified Public Accountants, New York.

prosper without sales. No bookkeeper or accountant is needed until some salesman brings in an order for goods or services. Accordingly, the major activity of the management of most small and medium-sized businesses is directed towards the sales and handling of customers' orders with the consequence that only a very minimum amount of attention is paid to the accounting phase. As a result, internal control, as such, is seldom given much thought or consideration and rarely any comprehensive planning in these businesses. The medium and smaller-sized company has neither the qualified staff available to set up such procedures nor does it have the same incentive for maintaining them, since there is no critical board of directors or stockholders checking management.

A basic principle of accounting control is that two or more people, who do not have access to the same records, act as a check upon one another. In many small offices where one, two, or three individuals must function in many capacities, it is simply impossible to provide all of the required checks. The system of internal control will make use of as many checks as possible under the circumstances, and the auditor will adjust his procedures accordingly.

One of the first steps in the audit program, as described in Chapter 1, is the examination of the system of internal control. A factor which the auditor must remain continually alert for is that no system will operate better than the people responsible for its operation. Accordingly, a system of internal control that may appear adequate on paper, may prove to be unsatisfactory in actual practice because it is not strictly adhered to. Accordingly, any change observed from the written procedure will be cause for the auditor to increase his tests and checks of the accounting records.

As a preliminary survey, many auditors use a questionnaire to check the various phases of internal control. Such a questionnaire has the obvious advantage of calling the attention of the auditor to certain sections which might otherwise be overlooked in the press of work. However, it is not practicable to design an internal control questionnaire which will cover every possible contingency. Therefore, a basic form of questionnaire is often used to develop salient points of the internal control system, so that additional investigation can be made in each area which indicates that such may be required.

Following is a suggested basic form of internal control questionnaire: It will be noted that this approaches the system of internal control from the standpoint of personnel, rather than from the standpoint of the various accounting functions. It is necessary, of course, that the various bookkeeping and accounting functions be related to the questionnaire, but the emphasis is primarily on the personnel of the client, since in the final analysis people are the element which makes the thing work.

Note: *This type of questionnaire has proved to be particularly useful in smaller companies where the office personnel is, for example, ten or less. When more than ten can be assigned to accounting and bookkeeping functions it is imperative that formal written accounting instructions be used. This number usually will easily provide sufficient personnel to properly allow the checks on the accounting procedures which are an integral part of the internal control system. It should be emphasized that ten is not necessarily a magical number and that in some instances fewer people in* *the office can also provide quite adequate control, depending upon the type of business and the assets being handled.*

INTERNAL CONTROL QUESTIONNAIRE

Note: *Use separate sheets if space is inadequate.*

Client:

Date of audit:

Date questionnaire prepared: *By:*

Reviewed by:

                                       Date:

General

No. of people in office: _____   No. exclusively in accounting: _____

Are there written instructions regarding the handling of accounting matters? _____

If there are written instructions, are they adequate under the circumstances? _____

Note: *Attach copy of instructions.*

Is there any evidence to show that management is aware of its responsibility to provide the best system of internal control under the circumstances?_____

Are basic managerial responsibilities spelled out, either in minutes or in other written documents? _____

Is each officer aware of his responsibilities in this area? _____

Is there an adequate organization chart, and is it followed? _____

Are minutes in proper form and up to date? _____

Are borrowings properly authorized by the board of directors? _____

Are funds resulting from borrowings deposited intact? _____

Are funds, including borrowings, received from sources other than remittances from customers properly protected? _____

Are budgets used:

     Sales? _____

     Operating costs? _____

Cash? _____

Fixed assets? _____

Management

Who is responsible for:

1. Accounting?

2. Product pricing?

3. Purchasing?

4. Signing checks?

5. Making bank deposits?

6. Approving customers' credit?

7. Approving journal entries?

8. Inventory control?

9. Maintenance?

10. Fixed assets purchases?

11. Securities, including notes receivable?

12. Collections?

13. Reviewing accounting procedures?

Accounting

List names of persons performing accounting functions:

A _____

B _____

C _____

D _____

E _____

F _____

G _____

H _____

I _____

J _____

Note: *Answer the following questions by filling in the letter assigned to the individual above.*

Who is responsible for:

1. Opening the mail? _____

2. Preparing cash receipts journal? _____

3. Entering customers' orders (sales journal)? _____

4. Entering customers' ledger debits (sales)? _____

5. Entering customers' ledger credits (payments)? _____

6. Preparing bank deposits? _____

7. Preparing customers' invoices? _____

8. Checking credit approval? _____

9. Preparing purchase orders? _____

10. Comparing receiving reports with vendors' invoices? _____

11. Entering vendors' invoices (purchase journal)? _____

12. Issuing vendors' checks? _____

13. Posting vendors' ledger credits (purchases)? _____

14. Posting vendors' ledger debits (payments)? _____

15. Preparing payroll checks? _____

16. Posting payroll entries to journal? _____

17. Posting payroll entries to detail earnings record? _____

18. Preparing journal entries? _____

19. Posting general ledger? _____

20. Preparing financial statements? _____

By using letters to indicate the personnel performing the various accounting functions, it will readily be apparent if there are duties which conflict with good internal control. Such a method will often show that changing a few positions may strengthen the system.

Obviously, the type of business will determine to a great extent the amount of internal control necessary. For example, finance companies are most vulnerable to manipulation by employees since they are handling the most volatile assets which a company has, namely cash. In the case of organizations which handle a great deal of consumer financing, either directly, such as consumer finance companies, or indirectly, such as mercantile businesses selling largely on the installment basis, it is necessary to spend far more time on cash and receivables. At the same time, because of the nature of the business, it is more common for such companies to have sufficient personnel in their accounting department to provide a much more formal and satisfactory system of internal control.

Since such organizations customarily borrow funds from banks and other sources, often pledging notes, contracts, and other receivables as security, the internal control system must take into consideration not only the receiving of cash but also the proper handling of all borrowings. There have been instances where a manager or owner of a consumer finance company, or other originator of consumer paper, has pledged the same assets to two or more lenders. With an adequate system of internal control, and ordinary audit procedures, such a situation should be easily and quickly discovered.

In businesses which originate consumer paper in fairly large amounts, such as automobile agencies and appliance dealers, there can be, in the absence of good internal control, an opportunity for "lapping." This is a term used to describe the action whereby an employee takes consumer paper, usually notes, conditional sales contracts, chattel mortgages, etc. to a bank or other financing agency and receives advances thereagainst. He then uses the money received on one day to replace money which he has borrowed earlier. In other words he can, by careful manipulation, have the use of substantial sums of money continuously by withholding the deposit of company funds for a period of time. The auditor must satisfy himself that the internal control system will not permit this to be done without exposure.

"Lapping" can also occur by simply depositing funds to an employee's own personal account, making them up at a later date with money received on that date. This can occur more easily when funds are received largely in cash, since checks are usually not accepted by a bank when made out to a corporation and deposited to the account of an individual. However, the author has seen checks which were endorsed by one corporation, although made out to another, and the error was not detected until the first company dunned the writer of the check for the amount of money due. Therefore, in a period where business activity is high and the banks are handling hundreds of thousands of checks each week, reliance should not be placed upon a bank teller to detect a fraudulent or erroneous endorsement.

It is the responsibility of the auditor to determine that the internal control system, as set up and operated by the client, is adequate to his needs. If it is not, then the auditor must undertake additional audit procedures to satisfy himself that the accounts are correct. It is advisable to write a letter to the client outlining the deficiencies in the client's system of internal control, and make suggestions as to how they may be overcome. The client is usually receptive to such a letter—first, because it may prevent an actual loss to the client, and secondly, by strengthening the internal control system it may ultimately reduce the audit fee. In addition, there is a very great moral responsibility, if not a legal responsibility on the part of the employer to avoid putting temptation in the way of his employees.

Many mechanical devices are in common use for providing some measure of internal control. For example, in retail establishments cash registers are in use. The use of a good cash register system can go a long way towards making the auditing of cash at the end of each employees' shift more accurate and in addition will furnish permanent written proof of the transactions. In auditing such an establishment, the first step of the internal control system would be to check carefully into the means of handling such cash transactions.

In addition to retail establishments, cash registers are adaptable for use with credit unions, savings and loan associations, insurance agencies, and in fact nearly any business which normally handles a large number of transactions daily. It is not practicable in a book of this size to go into all of the various types of equipment which are available, but the advent of more sophisticated data-control devices offers an excellent opportunity to improve accounting records.

While almost all larger corporations have a comprehensive bonding system in effect as well as insurance against loss by theft or defalcation, this is protection which is often lacking in the small and medium-sized companies. Examination of the bonds in effect, if any, are a part of the internal control examination, and if they are inadequate or if they are nonexistent, the auditor should take the precaution of notifying his client in writing to this effect.

The use of machine bookkeeping, and particularly the use of computers on either an installed or time-sharing basis has seen substantial recent development. Basically, there is no difference between auditing machine records and records compiled completely by handwritten methods. Mechanical problems, however, may arise. In the case of medium and small-sized businesses, it is customary for a print-out to be made of all of the material essential for a proper audit of the accounts. In fact, in most instances, the data thus generated permits an easier and more complete audit than do many hand methods. The exact procedures will depend upon the particular system being followed, and it will be necessary for the auditor to review the system as set up by the consultant or other person responsible for installation and/or operation of the system. Specific computer programs are being successfully used for auditing both the programming and the data of larger organizations, but are rarely practicable in auditing small and medium-sized organizations.

CLIENT'S REPRESENTATIONS

Inventory Certificate

An "Inventory Certificate" is a letter to the auditor signed by a responsible officer of the client certifying that the inventory has been counted, priced, etc. in accordance with the instructions. This in no way reduces the responsibility of the auditor for the thorough and proper verification of the inventory. It has, however, one desirable effect, that of calling attention once more to the fact that the financial statements are the financial statements of the client and not of the auditor. Not all auditors agree upon the use of the Inventory Certificate, but it does appear to have certain advantages, particularly among the small and medium-sized clients, in emphasizing their responsibility to conduct a proper inventory count and valuation. The auditor's work in verifying an inventory is made more effective and easier if the client insists that his employees make a thorough and satisfactory inventory count.

The Inventory Certificate is usually signed by the chief executive officer and the chief accounting officer, although there may be instances when a factory superintendent or some other official may be more appropriate, having more knowledge of the facts reported. Normally the "Certificate" would include the following information:

1. Date at which the inventory physical count was made, and extent of count.
2. Method of valuation used.
3. Method of determining quantity and value of obsolete, damaged, and slow moving goods.
4. Status of in-transit items (shipping and receiving).
5. Status and value of consigned merchandise (owned and nonowned), if any.
6. Liens or pledges of inventory, if any.

Liability Certificate

Similar to an "Inventory Certificate," a "Liability Certificate" is a signed statement by one or more officers of the client stating that all liabilities, both real and contingent, are reflected upon the books or disclosed to the auditor. Unlike inventory, which has substance and can be observed by the auditor, liabilities can be concealed rather easily if an officer and/or employee wish to do so. It is a simple matter for a file to be removed during the period that the auditor is on the client's premises. And while the Liability Certificate in no way diminishes the auditor's duty to properly verify and confirm liabilities, it does forcibly call to the client's attention his responsibility in this area. For this reason, Liability Certificates are nearly always obtained.

The Liability Certificate is usually signed by the chief executive officer of the organization, and by the treasurer, controller, or other financial officer. The following represents the minimum which would be included:

1. Statement that all liabilities have been recorded on the books.
2. That all contingent liabilities have been disclosed.
3. Title to all recorded assets lies with the organization.
4. All important items of equipment that have been sold, scrapped, abandoned, or otherwise disposed of during the year have been charged off of the books.
5. All purchase commitments have been disclosed.
6. Statement that any shortages or other irregularities discovered by the client during the year have been disclosed to the auditor.
7. A statement that between the audit date and the date of signing the "Certificate," no events have occurred that would materially affect the financial statements.

In addition, it appears appropriate in this connection to add a paragraph stating that the client understands the primary purpose of the examination has been to express an accountant's opinion on the fairness of the financial statements, and the examination will not necessarily disclose any irregularities, should such exist. This offers one more opportunity to emphasize the primary purpose of an audit, an objective with which the small and medium-sized client is not always completely familiar.

If desired, the two "Certificates" can be combined. This is especially convenient if the same officer or officers would normally sign both. The exact wording is not too important. Some auditing firms use a preprinted form, filling in the variable information, such as the total value of inventories. Other firms prefer to prepare a separate letter for each client, tailoring it to fit the specific conditions.

4

Auditing
Cash

The term "cash," as used in this chapter, is understood to include currency, coin, checks, money orders, and similar items. It does not include promissory notes and other negotiable instruments not payable on demand, and which cannot be deposited for immediate credit.

Cash represents the asset of an organization which can most easily be converted to unauthorized uses, and accordingly the audit of cash will represent a critical part of the auditor's examination. This is also the area where the system of internal control plays a most important role, and while this has been discussed in Chapter 3, the audit program for cash must be carefully prepared in light of the information revealed by the examination of the system of internal control.

Organizations usually fall into one of the two following categories with regard to their receipts of cash:

1. Receipts largely in the nature of currency, coin, numerous small checks, and money orders.

   Note: *In this category would be retail and service establishments dealing with the general public.*

2. Receipts largely in the form of checks, usually for larger amounts.

   Note: *This category would include manufacturers, wholesalers, brokers, and similar businesses.*

The audit program to be followed would depend to a large extent not only upon the system of internal control, but also into which area the business would fall.

AUDIT PROGRAM

Prior to Audit Date

1. Prepare a cash audit program.

    Note: *This is particularly important if there are a number of cashiers or cash register positions where cash must be counted.*

    Following is a suggested minimum cash audit program, which would be expanded if the system of internal control is not adequate:

Cash Audit Program

1. List each location where cash funds are held, showing for each, the date and time of the count, and name of staff member responsible.

    Note: *This would include office petty cash funds, cashiers' funds, drivers' change funds, cash register change funds, etc.*

2. On date listed above, take possession of cash box or drawer and cash register tapes, and/or other list of receipts and/or disbursements.

    Note: *It is essential that these be secured simultaneously. Common prudence dictates that all cash counts be made in the presence of the custodian and that a receipt be obtained from the custodian upon return of the cash. In the event of a first audit, it may be advisable to have a responsible officer of the company issue instructions to all employees affected as to the exact procedure to be followed by the auditor in making the cash count. Since such counts are preferably surprise counts, the instructions should be given to the auditor who in turn will present them to the custodian only at the time of the cash count.*

3. Count cash and enter on work sheet, listing all noncash items. Return cash to custodian, receiving a receipt for the return.

    Note: *This is one area where the use of a preprinted work sheet may save considerable time if there are a number of cash counts to be made.*

4. Cash register tapes or similar documents can usually be retained by the auditor until verification can be made and totals and other pertinent information entered on the work sheet.

5. Undeposited cash receipts on hand should be counted in the same manner.

6. Note number of last check used, and test to determine that all unused checks are accounted for and under adequate control.

Subsequent to Audit Date

1. Request direct confirmation from each depository of the balance to the client's credit as of the audit date.

Note: *It is advisable to mail bank confirmation requests as soon after the audit date as possible, so that there will be ample time for additional requests in the event that the first request is unanswered.*

2. Trace recorded cash receipts to the bank statement.

3. Reconcile bank accounts as of audit date.

   Note: *Reconciliations made by the client's bookkeeper for each month of the year under review should be examined to determine if there are any recurring unusual items. It is often advisable to make a cutoff reconciliation on a date subsequent to the audit date.*

4. Compare cancelled checks with cash disbursements journal.

   Note: *The number of months' checks to be compared will depend upon the system of internal control. The last month of the fiscal year is always done, and if a cutoff reconciliation is made, the checks written during that period would be compared. In some instances, it might be advisable to compare checks for the entire year if discrepancies are noted, or if internal control is lax.*

5. Prove footings of cash disbursements and cash receipts journals, and trace postings to general ledger.

   Note: *Again, the number of months for which this work is done will depend upon the internal control system and whether any discrepancies have been noted.*

6. Verify any journal entries made to the general ledger to determine that they are valid.

   Note: *Ordinarily, no entries are made to the general ledger cash in bank accounts, except from the cash receipts or cash disbursements journals.*

WORKING PAPERS REQUIRED

Cash Count

The work sheet showing the cash count is prepared by listing each denomination of bills and coins, showing the number of bills or coins and the total value for each. This is important in the event that any subsequent question should arise as to the count. Each noncash item is listed unless the number is very large, and the value of each is small, in which case an adding machine tape may be substituted if desired. Particular attention should be paid to any receipts representing loans or advances to employees or others. If such are discovered, they should be discussed with a responsible officer of the organization. The receipt, signed by the custodian of the cash fund counted, is usually a part of the work sheet for that particular fund, but may be a separate form if desired.

Comparison of Recorded Cash Receipts and Bank Deposits

There are a number of methods of accomplishing this procedure. The simplest, satisfactory for small organizations, is to compare each deposit as shown in the cash receipts book with the deposit shown on the bank statement. However, the volume of transactions in most audits does not make this a very practical solution.

The more common method is to prepare a work sheet—the first column listing months; the next column, total deposits for the month per the bank statement; next column, deposits in transit beginning of month; next column, deposits in transit end of month; next column, returned checks redeposited, but not recorded in the cash receipts journal; next column, for miscellaneous bank entries not recorded in the cash receipts journal, such as corrections of bank errors; last column, deposits for the month per general ledger. Figure 4-1 shows an example of this work sheet.

The above will satisfy the mechanical requirements of determining that all recorded cash receipts have been deposited to the credit of the client, but it will not disclose "lapping." Therefore, random tests of one or two months should be made to compare the date of the receipt of cash, as shown by the cash receipts journal, with the date the deposit was recorded by the bank. Any unexplained delays must be satisfactorily accounted for. In addition, selected day's deposits should be compared item by item. That is, each item on the bank's deposit slip should be compared with the items in the cash receipts journal, to determine that there has been no substitution of items. For example, if the cash book shows currency and coin amounting to $126.59, then exactly that amount should show on the bank deposit ticket. Checks received from the client's customers offer an even better opportunity for checking, since in most cases they will be for odd amounts. Any difference discovered in item detail is cause for further investigation. Since duplicate deposit slips can easily be prepared by an employee, only those bearing the bank's validation should be given credence. If the situation warrants, it may be necessary to visit the banks and examine their copies. Some banks make it a practice to return deposit slips as well as cancelled checks, and these offer a good source of verification. Complete notation of all verification of deposit dates and items should be entered on the work sheet.

Reconcile Bank Accounts

A work sheet should be prepared of the bank reconciliation as of the audit date, and, if such is done, at the cutoff date. The exact form is not too important, the following being the most commonly used:

Balance, per bank statement				10,000.00
Add: Deposit in transit				2,000.00
				12,000.00
Less: Outstanding checks:				
#1098	$100.00	#1200	$50.00	
1107	200.00	1201	50.00	
1145	100.00	1203	500.00	1,000.00
Balance per books				$11,000.00

XYZ CORPORATION
RECORDED CASH RECEIPTS AND BANK DEPOSITS
9-30-19XX

MONTH	DEPOSITS PER BANK STATEMENT	IN TRANSIT AT BEGINNING	IN TRANSIT AT END OF MONTH	RETURNED CHECKS REDEPOSITED	BANK ADJUSTMENTS	DEPOSITS PER GENERAL LEDGER
OCTOBER	10000 00	1000 00	4000 00	500 00	500 00	12000 00
NOVEMBER	12000 00	4000 00	2000 00	100 00	—	9900 00
DECEMBER	20000 00	2000 00	3000 00	1000 00	—	20000 00
SEPTEMBER	9000 00	2000 00	4000 00	700 00	100 00	10200 00
TOTAL	180000 00	26000 00	28000 00	12000 00	1000 00	169000 00

Figure 4-1

Outstanding checks and deposits in transit should be verified subsequent to the audit date by reference to the returned cancelled checks and the bank statement, respectively.

Compare Cancelled Checks

A work sheet should be prepared, showing the months for which cancelled checks were compared with the cash disbursements journal. Notation should be made of any discrepancies noted, and the disposition thereof. In examining cancelled checks, dates, payees, and amounts, signatures and endorsements should be noted. The auditor admittedly is not a handwriting expert, so he is not expected to detect forgeries. However, he should determine, from minutes and other evidence, who is authorized to sign checks on behalf of the client, and determine that only the names of those properly authorized appear on the cancelled checks.

A further problem appears in the matter of payroll checks. Endorsements on payroll checks are almost worthless from the standpoint of the auditor. If the organization is large enough so that the auditor is not familiar with each employee, he should take possession of all of the payroll checks for a selected payroll (which should be unannounced, and may be before or after the audit date), and personally distribute them to the employees. In this way, he has some opportunity of determining that they are legitimate, but room for manipulation still remains, so that all checks not delivered due to absence of employee must be carefully checked out.

Prove Footings and Trace Postings

A work sheet should be prepared showing the amount of verification done in this area.

Verification of Journal Entries

A work sheet should be prepared listing all journal entries made in the cash accounts in the general ledger, showing date, amount, and nature. Such journal entries should be discussed with a responsible official of the client, unless they were previously approved in writing by such an officer.

METHOD OF VERIFICATION

Cash in Bank

Verification of cash in banks is by direct correspondence with the depositories. Requests may be made by letter or the auditing firm's own form, but most auditors prefer to use the standard request for bank confirmation approved by the American Institute of Certified Public Accountants and the Association for Bank Audit Control and Operation. The requests must be signed by an officer of the client firm authorized to sign checks, and should be returned directly to the auditor's office.

Cancelled Checks

Arrangements should be made with the client's banks to have the last period's cancelled checks and bank statement mailed directly to the auditor's office, or, alternatively, have a representative of the auditor's office pick them up at the bank. This is the only way the auditor can be absolutely certain that he will receive the checks and statements intact.

It is axiomatic that all check numbers must be accounted for. Most bookkeepers have been instructed to retain voided checks, but if this has not been done and the voided checks are not available for examination, the auditor has reason to be suspicious. It is very difficult to determine if a check has cleared the bank and subsequently been destroyed if a substitute has been entered in the cash disbursements book and substitute check placed in the cancelled check file. When an auditor is looking at hundreds, perhaps thousands of cancelled checks, it is easy to overlook a reasonably well-prepared, forged cancelled check. The best security is to use prenumbered checks, keep the checks under strict control, and then verify that the unused sequence of numbers is intact.

REQUIREMENTS OF SPECIAL SITUATIONS

Handling of cash can create so many different special situations that it is not practicable to discuss them except in a very general way. Inevitably cash problems arise through an inadequate internal control system, which would not be limited to cash alone. As a very general rule, the smaller the organization usually the less formal the internal control system. The offsetting advantage, of course, is that the manager is much closer to the details of the business and therefore is usually more aware of any breakdown in controls. The only action that the auditor can take is to use extreme care in preparing his cash audit program and then be diligent in executing it.

Traditionally, the most junior accountants are given the task of comparing cancelled checks and other cash procedures. In conformity with the first standard of field work (that the work is to be adequately planned and assistants, if any, are to be properly supervised), such cash procedures handled by a junior accountant should be most carefully observed and guided. A sound rule would appear that the more inferior the system of internal control encountered, the more superior the auditing required.

FINANCIAL STATEMENT PRESENTATION

Presentation of cash on the balance sheet is usually very simple, since cash is one asset capable of being measured with considerable accuracy. Several different captions are favored, "Cash," "Cash on hand and in the banks," "Demand deposits," etc. The exact caption used will depend upon circumstances and the auditor's personal preference. As long as there is no room for misunderstanding, the caption used is probably not too important.

If the amount of cash on hand, such as change funds, office cash funds, etc, is significant, it is often shown separately. For example:

Demand deposits	$1,500	
Change funds (cash on hand)	1,000	$2,500

Cash is usually shown as the first item on the asset section of the balance sheet, since it represents the most current of the assets.

If the amount of cash in change funds or imprest cash funds represented by paid-out vouchers is significant, a journal entry should be made, charging the paid-outs to the proper expense or other account, and reducing cash by an equal amount. If the expense thus represented is very small, it is usually ignored and the entire amount shown as "Cash, on hand." For example, an organization has cash in bank (demand deposits), of $1,000 and an office imprest fund of $1,000, but in the imprest fund if $900 has been disbursed as a travel advance, it would be improper to show the cash on hand as $1,000. On the other hand, if the same organization showed demand deposits of $500,000 and imprest cash fund as above, most auditors would probably not reverse the amount of $900 representing the travel advance since it is insignificant when taken in connection with the total. From a strictly theoretical auditing viewpoint, however, every item in a cash account which is not cash should be reversed.

If there are any restrictions on the use of cash in banks, for example an agreement to retain a specified balance, it must be noted, either on the balance sheet itself or by a footnote. If there are no exceptions noted, the reader is entitled to assume that all cash shown on the balance sheet is unrestricted and available to the company for ordinary business purposes.

5

Auditing
Receivables

Receivables ordinarily constitute the largest single "quick asset," the liquidation of which is expected to provide funds for the payment of creditors; and proper classification of receivables is necessary to determine cash flow. Usual verification is by direct communication with debtors.

Trade receivables may be defined as amounts due from customers raising from sales of goods and services in the ordinary course of business. These amounts may be in the form of ordinary, unsecured, open accounts, or they may be in the form of notes, drafts, conditional sales contracts, or other instruments. In the case of contractors, they may represent earned partial or progress payments due on contracts.

For financial statement purposes, when volume justifies, receivables may be classified into one or more of the following categories:

- Accounts receivable—trade.
- Notes receivable—trade.
- Contracts receivable—trade.
- Progress payments receivable—trade.

In addition to trade receivables, a company may often have other receivables, such as advances to employees, officers, travel advances, amounts due from the sale of real estate or equipment not properly carried in inventory, rental from nonoperating property, and similar items. These "Receivables—Other" may be either current or noncurrent, depending upon the terms of sale. They must be segregated upon the financial statements even if they constitute current assets, and should not be combined with "Receivables—Trade."

AUDIT PROGRAM

As of Audit Date

1. Prepare trial balances of "Trade Receivables" with separate trial balances for each category, if required, and trial balance for "Receivables—Other."
2. Examine and compare with trial balance, all notes, drafts, contracts, and other documents, keeping them under control until examination has been satisfactorily completed.
3. Check cutoff of billing to determine that all shipments made have been billed, and that no shipments or deliveries of merchandise made subsequent to the audit date are included in receivables.

Subsequent to Audit Date

1. Mail requests for confirmation, after having checked requests to trial balance.
2. Compare detail receivable ledgers with trial balance.
3. Prove trial balance footings and aging.
4. Determine adequacy of write-offs or additions to bad debt reserve.
5. Compare returned confirmation requests with trial balance, and resolve any differences.
6. Follow up any confirmation requests not returned which are considered to be material.
7. Prepare and post to working trial balance, any necessary adjusting journal entries.
8. Prior to completing field work, enter on trial balance, all collections received subsequent to audit date. This provides additional confirmation of both the amount and the collectibility of receivables.

   Note: *There may be times when it is necessary to confirm receivables other than at the audit date. The same procedures would be followed as to requesting confirmations and other verification. In addition, it would be necessary to verify the transactions in the various receivable accounts from the date of the confirmation to the audit date.*

9. Eliminate all intercompany (if client has subsidiaries) and interdepartment or intersection accounts. It is rather uncommon for small and medium-sized clients to operate separate subsidiary corporations, but if such a situation does exist, it is essential that all intercompany accounts be eliminated for statement purposes.

WORKING PAPERS REQUIRED

Accounts Receivable

Prepare trial balance, showing name of debtor, amount due, and aging of accounts, as not yet due or past due. If accounts are past due, segregate by number of months past due. If receivables are pledged, indicate on the trial balance the accounts pledged, and to whom pledged. This will permit a later reconciliation with confirmation of payables. This is treated in more detail in Chapter 9, "Auditing Notes

Payable." Credit balances are shown separately, and it will be found more convenient if the credit balance column is the first column on the work sheet page following the name of the debtor. Figure 5-1 is an example of a satisfactory work sheet (page 66, 67).

Unless the total amount of customers' credit balances is very small, it must be reclassified as a liability for balance sheet purposes.

Notes Receivable

Prepare a trial balance, showing the name of debtor, amount due at audit date, amount of original note and terms, security, if any, date to which interest is paid, if applicable; also, show prepaid interest, accrued interest, amount due after one year, if any, and whether or not payments are current. Figure 5-2 (page 68, 69) depicts one method. If a detail note receivable ledger is maintained, it is compared with the trial balance.

As of the audit date, all notes, contracts, and other negotiable instruments must be examined by the auditor or placed under seal, to insure that all are properly accounted for and that no substitutions are made.

Any appreciable number of notes dated just prior to the audit date may well be considered suspicious. It is not uncommon for notes, otherwise delinquent, to be renewed just prior to the audit date in order to show a better current position. If such a situation is discovered it must be thoroughly investigated, and full disclosure made when required by the facts.

Contracts Receivable

Prepare trial balance, similar to that for "Notes Receivable."

Receivables—Other

Prepare trial balance for any receivables not included in the foregoing. In addition, information should be provided to indicate the nature of the receivables, such as travel advance, employee's advance, etc. Space should be provided for classifying into current and noncurrent if applicable.

Bad Debts Reserve (or Write-Off)

A corollary to receivables is the provision for bad debts. A work sheet will be required to show how the bad debt allowance was determined. If the client is on the reserve basis, it will be necessary to show the amount added to the reserve, and the amounts charged thereagainst. If a write-off method is used, the accounts written off must be reviewed. It will be necessary to review previous years' provisions for comparison purposes. Any material change in ratio of charge-offs to sales and receivables from one year to the next must be thoroughly investigated to determine the cause.

In auditing this area, reference will be made to the aging of the receivables, so that an opinion may be formed as to the adequacy of the bad debt allowance. Past due

X Y Z CORPORATION
9 - 30 - 19XX
ACCOUNTS - RECEIVABLE - TRADE

	CREDIT BALANCE	DEBIT TOTAL	NOT YET DUE	PAST DUE 1-30	31-60
ABLE CONSTRUCTION		100000	75000	25000	
BAKER MATERIALS		50000	50000		
CATLIN MFG.	400				
DAVIS BROS.		95000	40000	40000	10000
DUGGAN, INC.		35000	35000		
ERIN, LTD		500000	500000		
FRANK AND FRANK		65000	60000		5000
TOTALS	50400	2500000	2150000	200000	90000

Figure 5-1

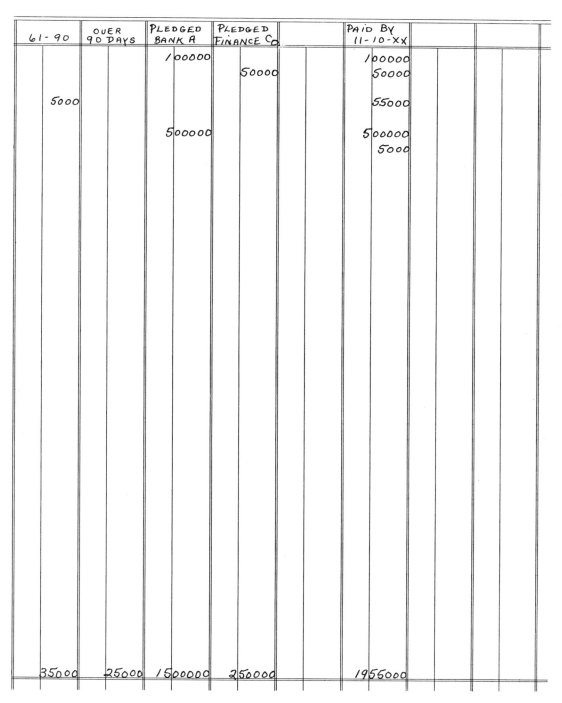

61-90	OVER 90 DAYS	PLEDGED BANK A	PLEDGED FINANCE Co.		PAID BY 11-10-XX			
		100000			100000			
			50000		50000			
5000					55000			
		500000			500000			
					5000			
35000	25000	1500000	250000		1955000			

Figure 5-1 (contd.)

XYZ CORPORATION
9-30-19XX
NOTES RECEIVABLE-TRADE

NAME	SECURITY	TERMS	ORIGINAL	DUE	INTEREST RATE
ANDERSON & CO.	NONE	6 MONTHS	4-15-19XX	10-15-19XX	6 %
BAKER & SON	CHATTLEMTG. (MACHINERY)	12 INSTALLMENTS 270⁰⁰/MO	6-1-19XX	6-1-19XX	$8 ADD ON
JONES & SMITH	CONDITIONAL	36 INSTALLMENTS 98³³/MO	3-1-19XX	3-1-19XX	$6 ADD ON

Figure 5-2

ORIGINAL AMOUNT	DUE 9-30-19XX	PRINCIPAL 12 MONTHS	DUE AFTER 12 MO.	INTEREST PREPAID	ACCRUED	NOTES:	
500000	500000	500000	-0-	-0-	13750	INTEREST - 5½ MONTHS	
324000	243000	243000	-0-	INCLUDED		CURRENT	
354000	304833	118000	186833	INCLUDED		DELINQUENT	1 MONTH
2150000	1540000	580000	960000	25000	67500		

Figure 5-2 (contd.)

receivables are obviously of questionable collectibility. Past company experience, however, is usually a good indication of the ultimate collections to be expected. Large amounts should be investigated individually. It is rather rare for small businesses to carry credit insurance, but if such insurance is carried, it should be considered in determining the bad debt allowance. It is advisable to look at the correspondence files of attorneys and collection agencies regarding specific receivables, and correspondence pertaining to all accounts written off should be examined to determine that the account should, in fact, be written off. All reference to amounts collected on accounts previously charged off, should be traced to the cash receipts book to verify that they have been properly accounted for.

METHOD OF VERIFICATION

Trade Accounts Receivable

Statements of account are prepared by the client (the client's usual monthly statement is satisfactory for this purpose), are checked against the trial balance for accuracy (indicating clearly on the work sheet those statements for which verification is being requested), the auditor's confirmation request is applied, and the statements then deposited in the mail by the auditor or under his direct control. If statements are mailed in the client's envelopes, it is important that his name be blocked out and the auditor's name applied, so that in the event of nondelivery by the post office, they will be returned to the auditor and not to the client. During the preparation of requests for confirmation, statements must remain under the complete control of the auditor.

Requests for confirmation may be either "negative," in which case the recipient is asked to notify the auditor if the statement is *not* correct, or "positive," in which case the recipient is asked to sign the statement, stating that the amount shown is correct, or if not correct, to explain any difference. In the case of a "positive" request for confirmation, a stamped envelope addressed to the auditor must be included. It is apparent that 100 per cent compliance with requests for a "positive" confirmation cannot be expected. Accordingly, the auditor must make additional requests for confirmation to those not responding to the original request. Even with such a follow-up, some requests will nearly always remain unanswered. The auditor must then determine whether or not they are significant. If the amounts are substantial, or there is some other reason to insist upon a confirmation, a telephone call by an officer of the client company will usually produce results.

In the case of companies with a relatively small number of accounts, it is advisable to confirm all accounts, using a negative request, except for those accounts selected because of size or other conditions, which are to be sent positive requests. In case of a client having hundreds of accounts receivable, where it is not practicable to confirm all receivables, select all of those over a specific amount, for example $50 or $100 (to provide confirmation of the largest amount of total receivables), and select a sample of all others, perhaps one of each ten remaining. However, if the client regularly sends out monthly statements, it is much more satisfactory to confirm all such accounts, since the extra cost of doing so is negligible.

Following is a sample of a satisfactory request for a negative confirmation. This may be in the form of a rubber stamp or a printed gummed sticker, the latter being preferred by many auditors.

AUDITOR'S VERIFICATION

Please examine this statement. It will be assumed that this statement is correct unless you contact our auditors.

Able, Baker, and Carr
Certified Public Accountants
1000 Central Avenue
Our Town, State

Please write and list details of any differences.

Positive requests are often made on the auditor's printed forms, without the client's authorizing signature. Since there is no way for the recipient to know that the request is legitimate, it is often ignored. In the writer's opinion, no confirmation request should be used, unless it is on the client's stationery, and/or signed by a responsible officer.

Following is a commonly used form:

Gentlemen:

Our auditors, Able, Baker, and Carr, Certified Public Accountants, 1000 Central Avenue, Our Town, State, are now engaged in their regular examination of our accounts as at September 30, 19xx. According to our records, you were indebted to us as follows on September 30, 19xx:

Open Account $

If this agrees with your books, will you please sign in the space below and return in the enclosed envelope. If the amount does not agree, will you please explain the differences.

Your cooperation is greatly appreciated.

Very truly yours,

XYZ Corporation

By _____

The amount shown above is correct:

(Signed) _____

If *not* correct, please explain the differences below:

Governmental agencies almost universally ignore confirmation requests, so that if there are significant amounts in this category, other means of satisfying himself must be used by the auditor. Often correspondence in the client's files will contain sufficient information in this respect. In other cases, subsequent payment may be used as verification. In the case of significantly large amounts due on government contracts, it is sometimes possible to work directly with the contracting officers to secure a confirmation of the accounts. Failing this, the auditor may find it necessary to modify his opinion, or in the case of minor amounts, to footnote the financial statements.

Notes Receivable

A letter prepared and signed by the client is mailed by the auditor, following the general procedure used for accounts receivable. It is usually more satisfactory to have the pertinent information put in the letter by the client's staff, rather than expecting the maker of the note to do so. It is much easier for the recipient of the confirmation request to check and to approve than it is to look up the original data and put it on the confirmation request. This results in more confirmation requests being returned to the auditor.

Following is one form of letter frequently used:

Gentlemen:

In connection with our regular audit, will you please confirm directly to our auditors Able, Baker, and Carr, Certified Public Accountants, 1000 Central Avenue, Our Town, State, the following information regarding promissory note(s) made by you and held by us as of September 30, 19xx:

> Date of note.
> Original amount of note.
> Interest rate.
> Security (if any).
> Date due (or installments due).
> Principal amount unpaid at September 30, 19xx.
> Date to which interest has been paid.

This information is for audit purposes only, and is not a request for payment. Your prompt reply in the enclosed stamped, addressed envelope will be greatly appreciated.

Very truly yours,

XYZ Corporation

By _____
President

The above information is correct:

Signed: _____

Date _____

The above information is *not* correct. Following is an explanation of differences:

While the above letter is satisfactory when sent to business houses, a different form is recommended when the letters are addressed to the average consumer. As compared to results from confirmation requests sent to business organizations, requests sent to individuals are often ignored because the average person is unaware of the nature or the purpose of the confirmation. Since notes and contracts must be confirmed, wording for requests to individuals may well be expanded to explain the reason for the request.

Such a letter may be worded along the following lines:

To Our Customers:

We are having our regular audit made by Able, Baker, and Carr, Certified Public Accountants, 1000 Central Avenue, Our Town, State, and as a part of their regular audit procedure it is necessary for them to ask you to confirm directly to them that the amount which we show you owing us on our books, as of *September 30, 19xx,* is correct.

On September 30, 19xx, according to our records, you owed a total of _____, payable in installments with _____ dollars per month due on the _____ of each month. As of September 30, 19xx, our records show that all payments were made that were due except _____ (if any).

If you agree with this, will you please sign below and return in the stamped, addressed envelope enclosed. This is not a request for payment, and please *do not* send money to our auditors.

Your cooperation is appreciated.

Very truly yours,

XYZ Corporation

By _____

The above information is correct.

Signed: _____

Date _____

The above information is *not* correct. Following is an explanation of differences:

REQUIREMENTS OF SPECIAL SITUATIONS

Peculiar problems arise in connection with the verification of receivables in certain lines of business endeavor. The following list is intended to be indicative of those encountered in auditing medium-sized clients, but is not intended to be definitive.

Financial Organizations

This would include consumer finance companies, savings and loan associations, credit unions, and banks. In this situation, receivables represent the largest part of the total assets of the organization and accordingly a larger portion of the auditor's time will usually be spent on the verification of accounts and notes receivable than in a trading or manufacturing concern. Certain of these institutions have statutory requirements for audits with which the auditor is presumed to be familiar.

In the case of consumer finance companies in particular, great care must be observed in the selection of accounts and notes to be verified in the event that there is not a 100 per cent verification, and the auditor must conduct with greatest care his examination of the actual notes and contracts to satisfy himself that they constitute a proper asset.

It is rather common practice for certain financial concerns to pledge or discount receivables. If receivables are sold without recourse, a rather rare situation, there is, of course, no contingent liability and no asset account will appear for those sold. If receivables have been pledged or assigned, however, the resulting liability must be verified by the auditor. Requirements for assigning or pledging receivables vary in different jurisdictions, but in most cases the account receivable or note receivable detail ledger sheet is suitably marked. As the various receivable trial balances are compared with the detail ledger sheets, a notation should be made on the trial balance of the amount shown to be pledged, and if there is more than one pledgee, which pledgee has the receivable. Auditing the liability is treated in detail in Chapter 9, "Auditing Notes Payable."

Service Organizations

Some service organizations with no inventories, such as insurance agencies, often report on a cash basis. Financial statements based upon a cash basis of reporting do not reflect the financial position of a company at a given period, unless by coincidence. Nominally, cash basis operations have no receivables to confirm, but since it is almost always necessary to convert to an accrual basis to prepare acceptable financial statements, receivables must be confirmed in the usual manner.

Contractors

Receivables of contractors usually will contain "retentions" which represent amounts withheld from payment on contracts, pending final acceptance of the job.

While these normally represent a legally enforceable claim, there may be a contingent liability for warranty work, so that a full explanation must be made on the financial statements. Confirmation of retentions must be made by direct correspondence, using a "positive" confirmation request. In addition to retentions, contractors often have progress or partial billings for work in progress. These also should be confirmed directly with debtors, using a "positive" confirmation request.

Utilities

Utility accounts are billed periodically, usually monthly, as long as a customer uses the service. Payments are made accordingly, and if payment is not made as specified, service is discontinued. This provides a satisfactory manner of checking the validity of the average householder account, and since requests for confirmation to such consumers are seldom satisfactory in any event, direct confirmations are seldom used. All very large accounts, and any that appear to be out of the ordinary course of business, should be sent positive confirmation requests.

FINANCIAL STATEMENT PRESENTATION

Current trade receivables are segregated by type, that is, accounts, notes, contracts, progress billings, etc., and shown in the current asset section of the balance sheet. If material in amount, they should be further separated by those receivables that are secured and those that are unsecured. Any receivables which have been pledged to secure payment of debts must be noted, either on the balance sheet itself or in footnotes. Other (nontrade) receivables may be lumped together under one caption if small in amount, except that amounts due from officers and/or stockholders should be noted, either as a separate caption on the financial statements or as a footnote.

Noncurrent receivables, segregated by type if the amounts are material, should be shown with "Other Assets" on the balance sheet.

The allowance for bad debts, if such an account is maintained, is usually shown as a deduction from the total amount of receivables, with a separate amount for current and for noncurrent receivables. However, if significant, a separate reserve can be shown for each class of receivables, both current and noncurrent.

Banks and other credit grantors are particularly interested in the aging of receivables. Accordingly, in the Supplemental Information portion of the audit report, a summary of the aging should be presented. It is more useful if a comparison with prior years can be given. On the adjacent page is an example showing how to make a summary-of-aging-receivables entry on the audit report.

A very brief summary of verification procedures may also be included, as well as a note as to the amount of collections received between the audit date and completion of field work. If there have been significant changes in the amount of bad debt write-offs from prior years, this should be noted, together with the amounts involved.

| | 19xx | | September 30, 19xy | | 19xz | |
	Amount	%	Amount	%	Amount	%
Not yet due	5,000	50	6,000	55	4,000	44
Past due 1–30 days	3,000	30	3,000	27	3,000	33
Past due 30–60 days	1,500	15	1,000	9	1,700	19
Past due over 60 days	500	5	1,000	9	300	4
Total	10,000	100	11,000	100	9,000	100

6

Auditing
Inventories

Inventories may be roughly grouped into one of three general categories:

1. *Retail inventories,* usually consisting of relatively small quantities of a substantial number of different items, such as those found in a drugstore, a hardware store, or a department store.

2. *Wholesale inventories,* which may also run into a fairly large number of different items, but the quantities of each item are greater than those of a retailer, and are generally in large containers, making them much easier to count.

3. *Manufacturer's inventories,* which will usually consist of raw material, goods in process, and finished goods.

Of these three general categories, the first two are relatively easy to check and price, although the sheer quantity may present some physical problems, but the third category involves the problem of pricing partially manufactured goods which in turn requires an allocation of factory burden.

The auditor's basic responsibility with regard to verification of inventories, is to be present at the time that the client's employees are making the inventory count, to observe the method used, to make tests and checks as to the accuracy of the count made by the client's employees, to satisfy himself that all inventory which should properly be included has been included, and to verify the valuation and the mechanical extension and footings of the inventory.

The significance of inventories as a portion of total current assets will vary greatly with different business enterprises. For a retailer, wholesaler, or manufacturer, inventories may well represent from 50 to 80 per cent of the total; for service organizations such as hotels and motels, restaurants, insurance, and real estate agencies, etc. they are minimal. Accordingly, the auditor in planning his audit will give due consideration to the relative importance of the inventories.

During the fiscal period, book inventories are computed by adding purchases to the opening inventory, adjusting for purchase returns and allowances, and subtracting the cost of goods sold. Cost of goods sold, in turn, is usually computed by using a percentage of sales. At the end of the fiscal period (the audit date), inventories must be verified so that the book inventory can be corrected, by making a physical count of the items comprising the inventory. This is the method most commonly used by small and medium-sized businesses, and the audit procedures are based upon this premise. However, perpetual inventories are occasionally used, and modifications of the audit program to cover this method of inventory keeping are explained at the end of this chapter under "Requirements of Special Situations."

AUDIT PROGRAM

Prior to Audit Date

1. Review with the client all of the locations where inventory is stored and agree as to the dates upon which the count will be made by the client's employees. In the case of multiple locations, it is important that the auditor assign sufficient of his staff so that the inventory observation and check can be made promptly. In the case of a manufacturer, it is almost imperative that operations be stopped for the purpose of the inventory count. It is extremely difficult to get a satisfactory count if operations continue and material continues to move from one location to another. If it is not possible to shut down operations completely, then the auditor will have to be doubly sure that proper segregation of material can be made long enough for it to be counted.

2. Secure a copy of the client's instructions to his employees for making the inventory count, and ascertain that the procedures are acceptable for a satisfactory inventory count.

   Note: *With small and medium-sized clients, it will often be found that the client himself does not have the knowledge and experience required to prepare inventory instructions. It then becomes the obligation of the auditor to confer with the client, to the end that satisfactory instructions can be made and can be given to all employees and supervisors involved.*

Following is one set of instructions, primarily for use in a manufacturing concern, which can be used as a basic guide. With certain modifications it can be applied equally to a retail or wholesale operation. Again, it should be pointed out that this represents a general outline, and specific instructions should be included to cover particular circumstances.

INSTRUCTIONS FOR INVENTORY COUNT

A physical count of all finished goods, work in progress, and raw material will be made starting Monday morning, September 30, 19xx. The plant will cease all operations for the purpose of taking inventory. Assignment of personnel will be the responsibility of John Doe, Superintendent.

As in prior years, inventory tags will be used. One tag must be used for each item or group of the same items. For example, if 12 cases of ½ inch gadgets, part #1234, are stacked together, only one card will be necessary for all 12 cases. If, however, the same item is in more than one location, a separate inventory tag will be required for each location.

Cards will be issued by serial numbers and all cards must be accounted for. If a card is spoiled or voided, the entire card must be returned. Each supervisor or group leader to whom inventory tags are issued, will be responsible for the serial numbers of all tags issued to him.

Start at one corner of the designated area, and work down one aisle, and then back, proceeding directly from one aisle to the next, without skipping. If in doubt as to whether an item is to be counted, make out a tag and mark it with the appropriate description, such as "scrap," "obsolete," or something similar.

The description must be entered on each card, and the description must be sufficient so that each item can be identified easily. In the case of work in progress, the shop order number should be put on the inventory tag and the last operation performed should be indicated. The proper spaces for all information are identified on the printed card.

In the "amount" box, enter the number of items in the particular group. Also indicate the unit; that is, whether the count is by units, weight, or in the case of packaged material, cases, indicating the quantity of each item per case.

It is not necessary to make any entries on the stub portion of the card. Do not detach the card from the stub. When information has been entered on the card, attach the stub to the item or to the first one of a group of items. These may be attached by means of staples, wire ties, or pressure tape. Do not remove any cards until authorized to do so by our auditors.

Start with the lowest number in the group of cards assigned and do not skip any cards.

Representatives of our auditors will be present during the inventory count and will be making tests and checks of the accuracy of the count. At the conclusion of your assigned area, report to the office of the superintendent and turn in all unused inventory tags.

As of Audit Date

1. Check receiving reports, or in the absence of formal receiving reports check such records as the company may maintain to show the receipt of merchandise, so that a proper cutoff can be made. It is important to determine that all of the material to be counted in the inventory has been received on or before the audit date, and that no inventory is included which will be shipped prior to the close of business on the audit date. Reference to shipments will be made by inspecting copies of invoices, shipping papers, bills of lading, or other data. This same information will also be used in verifying accounts receivable and accounts payable.

2. Observe the actual count being made and make test checks as to its accuracy. If inventory tags (preferably with a stub which can be left with the material) are used, this is relatively simple. The auditor can start in any area and see for himself that each item or group of items which should be counted is tagged. At this time he will be alert to be sure that nothing has been overlooked, and that no item has been counted twice. By reference to the quantity shown on the inventory tag, he can recount the item to see that the quantity shown is correct. At the beginning the items will be checked very frequently, perhaps every two or three items, and if the auditor is satisfied that there are no errors, a much smaller sample can be used for the remainder. In this connection it is important to check items with the greatest possible value, as an error in this area may result in a fairly substantial error; whereas, a difference of count where the total value is small has little effect on the total inventory valuation. If the inventory count is made on inventory sheets, a practice which is quite common among very small companies, particularly retailers, the problem of the auditor is somewhat greater, since it is more difficult to determine from such sheets whether or not all items have been included which should have been included. If substantial errors are noted, the auditor will have to confer with management, to determine whether or not the inventory should be recounted. While it is the client's primary responsibility to see that a correct count is made, the auditor has the responsibility of satisfying himself that in fact a proper and satisfactory count actually has been made. During the observation of the inventory count, the auditor must be alert to see that scrap, obsolete, or unsalable material is plainly identified on the inventory records, so that proper allowance can be made.

3. After the auditor has satisfied himself that the count is substantially correct, if tags are used, the tags can be pulled, sorted by number, and all issued numbers accounted for. All missing tags must be located. A sample listing of tags should be made, preferably representing a substantial part of the total value of the inventory, for later checking back against the client's completed inventory.

Subsequent to Audit Date

1. Upon receipt by the auditor of the inventory report, he should compare his notes made at the time he was observing the inventory count to see that the items that he noted appear correctly on the inventory sheet. Again, in this connection, it is important to pick the items of the greatest value. It will often be found, for example, that as high

as 30 to 40 per cent of the total value of an inventory can be traced from the physical inventory count to the final inventory valuation. Any discrepancies must be satisfactorily resolved.

2. Test-check the pricing of the inventory. A retail establishment will normally use the retail pricing method. This is simply that the items are all priced at retail and then the various groups having the same basic discount are totalled and the discount applied to obtain the cost. For example in a drugstore, all items with a customary 50 per cent markup (on cost) would be totalled by retail price and a 33⅓ per cent discount applied, reducing the retail value to average cost. It is obvious that there will be minor discrepancies, but if properly done the differences will be immaterial. While checking the inventory count, the auditor will also have verified the retail price which is normally marked upon the item itself or upon the shelf, so that it is fairly simple by checking the vendor's invoice to determine the markup. The auditor will check a sufficient number of items to satisfy himself that there is a consistent pattern which is correctly priced. If a substantial variation is noted, it may be necessary to regroup the items according to their actual markup.

Wholesale pricing would normally be at cost, the cost being verified by reference to vendor's invoices.

Manufacturers: Raw material is normally priced at cost which can be verified by reference to vendor's invoices. In arriving at the cost of work in process and finished goods, it will be necessary for the auditor to review the cost system used by the client to determine that the method is a reasonable and proper one. The greatest problem usually arises in the allocation of factory burden. It should also be determined that no general and administrative expense or selling expense is included in arriving at manufactured costs.

The method of inventory valuation most commonly used by small businesses is "first in, first out." If, however, the company should use a "last in, first out" or some other method of determining inventory, it will be necessary to verify that the pricing is in conformity with the method used.

3. The extensions and footings should be test-checked sufficiently to satisfy the auditor that they are correct. If any discrepancies at all are noted, a further checking should be made to determine the extent of the errors. If errors are fairly frequent, it may be necessary to have the entire inventory rechecked by the client's employees. It will of course be necessary for the auditor to again test the corrected inventory to determine that the recheck has been satisfactory. Usually footings would be verified in detail, unless the inventory ran to hundreds of sheets (unusual for small businesses). If an inventory summary has been prepared it will be traced back to the detail inventory sheets, and if not, the auditor will prepare his own summary.

WORKING PAPERS REQUIRED

Inventory Count

Prepare work sheets, the number depending upon the extent of the inventory, with the following headings:

1. Tag number (if tags are used) or sheet number (if sheets are used).
2. Part number (if used).
3. Description of item.
4. Last operation and job order number (if used) for work in process.
5. Client's count.
6. Auditor's count.

> **Note:** *Location of inventory should be indicated on work sheets, such as "Building A" or "Housewares Department," if such is needed to identify the area.*

Figure 6-1 shows a satisfactory form.

As the auditor starts his checking, usually after one entire area has been completely counted, he will enter information as listed above, except for "Auditor's Count." He will then count the item and enter his count in the appropriate column. If there is a discrepancy, he will recount to be sure that he, himself, has made a correct count. If he finds that he is correct and the tag is wrong, he would then count the next item. If the second item checks out correctly, he might skip two or three items before making the next check. If subsequent checks prove satisfactory, he might well ignore the first count, although he would correct the amount shown on the tag.

In selecting items to be checked, the auditor will always try for the largest total value. For example, he would choose to test-check the count of 1,000 items with a value of $10 each, rather than 1,000 items worth 10 cents each.

It is not possible to set any arbitrary standard for the amount of checking of the inventory count. However, some guidelines may be useful, remembering that these are for small and medium-sized businesses.

For the purposes of illustration, assume that the total inventory value is $100,-000, and consists of about 1,000 different items of varying unit cost. The auditor can ascertain from previous inventory records, or by discussion with client's personnel if it is a first audit, that approximately 20 per cent of the items account for 80 per cent of the total dollar value. It would probably be quite practicable to verify the count on at least one-half of the 20 per cent portion, thus accounting for 40 per cent or more of the total actual inventory value. The remaining 80 per cent would be thoroughly spot-checked, and of course the inventory would be checked for scrap, obsolete, and slow moving items to be sure that they are properly identified on the inventory records.

The auditor would also check to see that the inventory instructions are being properly carried out. When the auditor has verified that the count is substantially correct and that the inventory instructions are being followed, he can release the inventory and, if tags are used, pull the tags himself, or have employees of the client do so under his direct supervision. In some cases where the inventory is relatively small, it may be practicable to pull the inventory tags as he covers the area.

Inventory Instructions

A copy of the inventory instructions should be filed with the working papers.

X Y Z COMPANY
9-30-XX

BUILDING A   COUNT

	TAG #	PART #	ITEM	LAST OPERATION JOB #	CLIENT	OUR
	4601	46A	BRACE	2727	80	79
	4603	221	WHEEL	3027	121	121
	4605	107	WHEEL	1907	148	148

Figure 6-1

Last Invoice and Last Receiving Report

A work sheet should be made showing the number of the last sales invoice used so that it will be possible to verify that all items shipped have been billed and thus included in sales, and that they have not been included in the inventory. Similarly, the last receiving report should be noted so that it can be verified that all merchandise received by the audit date has been included in inventory and in accounts payable.

In-Transit Items

A work sheet should be prepared showing invoice number, vendor, date shipped, and invoice amount for all material shipped prior to the audit date, but not received until after the inventory has been counted. This will often be true of material shipped by rail, where normal transit time may run a week or more. Receipts for the month or so following the audit date should be checked to insure that all in-transit items are accounted for. In this connection, freight charges should not be overlooked. If the vendor's invoice is picked up in accounts payable, and the client is responsible for the freight, the amount of freight must be included in accounts payable, since the cost of freight will automatically be included in the inventory value.

Cost, Extensions, and Footings

A work sheet will be prepared showing items selected for verification of cost by comparison with vendor's invoices (or with cost records if a manufactured inventory). Again, the auditor should be aware of the relative value of the items, and check particularly those with a high value. It is also good practice to check items with a large quantity, even though the unit cost is low. Occasionally the unit price can be in error, and if there is a large quantity the total error could be significant. Full notation should be made on the work sheets indicating the number of items checked, the method used, and the results: no errors, few errors, or many errors. Instead of making up work sheets for this purpose, it is often practicable to make a copy of the client's inventory sheets and write the necessary notations on them.

Consigned Inventories

A work sheet should be prepared showing the location of any inventory material on consignment to a customer, which has not been invoiced, and which remains the property of the client. The work sheet should show the location, name of consignee, and total value of the consignment. If there has been a memorandum billing, the date and reference number of the memorandum billing should be noted.

Upon occasion, a client may have on his own premises material received on consignment from a vendor. In such an event, a work sheet should be prepared showing for each consignment the consignor, memo billing reference numbers, and a brief description of the items, together with their value.

Inventory Summary

A summary is prepared from the client's inventory sheets, showing the total inventory value for each major category. This summary (page 88) should also show the percentage of the inventory checked from physical count to completed inventory, percentage of pricing verified, and if the footings were not verified in full, the percentage checked. It would be appropriate to comment generally on the inventory count as observed by the auditor.

METHOD OF VERIFICATION

Purchased Material

Almost all inventory carried by a wholesaler or retailer, and raw material in the case of a manufacturer, will consist of purchased material. The cost will be determined by reference to vendor's invoices, with attention being given to dates, depending upon whether the client is using a "first in, first out" or "last in, first out" method of valuation, or some other method. Terms of the vendor's invoices should be carefully noted, particularly to determine whether or not freight is included. If freight is paid on incoming shipments by the buyer, the auditor should determine that freight has been included in the cost.

Work in Process and Finished Goods

The auditor will have to make a careful review of the method of cost used by the client. Normally many items included in factory burden will have been subjected to checking during the course of the audit. These will include labor, payroll taxes and insurance, rent, depreciation, repairs, and property taxes and insurance, which comprise most of the elements making up factory burden, thus providing a good audit of this area of manufacturing cost.

Consigned Inventory

Inventory, property of the client, which has been consigned to a customer, should be verified by direct correspondence with the consignee. If located in the same city, and if it is material in amount, in addition to confirming the ownership in writing, the inventory itself can be observed by the auditor. In the case of consumer goods, certain legal formalities may be required in some jurisdictions to insure that title remains with the consignor, so the auditor should check to insure that these formalities have been complied with.

XYZ Company
9-30-19XX
Inventory Summary

					% Verified	
					Count	Price
Raw Material	Dept	A	18600		42	60
" "		B	42100		36	81
" "		C	7900		24	30
Total			68600		36	69
In Process	Dept	A	16200		35	55
" "		B	21600		40	60
" "		C	2400		20	30
Total			40200		37	56
Finished Goods	Dept	A	24000		51	60
" "		B	52400		45	75
" "		C	12600		32	50
Total			89000		45	69
Factory Supplies			15000		15	20
Total Inventory			212800		38	63

Remarks:
    Count - Satisfactory - Very Few Errors
    Pricing - Excellent - No Significant Errors

Figure 6-2

In the case of consigned inventory on the premises of the client, it is important to insure that none has been included in the client's inventory. Confirmation should be requested from the consignor, verifying that it is a consignment and not a sale, terms of the consignment, general description of the items, and total value. If any special terms are imposed, such as insurance coverage, the auditor should verify that such conditions have been met.

REQUIREMENTS OF SPECIAL SITUATIONS

The nature of inventories encountered in the audit of small and medium-sized businesses is almost limitless, and will encompass the entire range of American business, from the exotic to the mundane, from vanilla beans to scrap iron. The same basic audit principles apply to each. However, there are some obstacles to getting a satisfactory count of some inventories. For example, scrap metal found in metal processors such as foundries, refiners, etc. cannot be accurately weighed (except at a prohibitive cost), so the auditor must rely upon management's estimates, comparison with prior year's inventories, costs, and sales. If the amount is significant, an outside appraiser may be used. Similarly, when items of high value, not readily identifiable, such as precious metals and gems, comprise an appreciable part of the inventory, the auditor would be compelled to rely upon the valuation of an outside independent appraiser. The auditor is not expected to be an appraiser or valuer, and is, therefore, entitled to rely upon outside opinions. The auditor does have the responsibility, however, to select an outside expert who is completely independent and who is competent.

Material in public warehouses in the past has been verified by examining official warehouse receipts. In view of recent developments, there is some question as to whether or not this is entirely satisfactory. At the minimum, such receipts should be confirmed directly with the public warehouse. If the amount warehoused is manufactured or identifiable material, and is significant in amount, it can be viewed at the warehouse. In the case of unidentifiable products, such as grain or petroleum products, confirmation of the warehouse receipts appears to be the only practicable method of verification.

Some retail businesses present difficulties in obtaining a good inventory count because first, it is difficult or impossible to completely close down for more than a weekend (if that), and secondly because of the multiplicity of items to be counted and valued. Among these are franchised automobile dealers' parts departments, supermarkets, hardware stores, and department stores. During the past few years, a number of organizations have come into being who specialize in making an inventory count and valuation for businesses of this type. Because they are specialists, they can usually make a count very much faster than the client's employees; hence, they are often employed where time is a factor. While the auditor can usually place more reliance upon the information developed by independent outside organizations than by members of the client's staff, it should be emphasized that this in no way relieves him of his basic responsibility to observe and test the inventory count.

Although not often encountered among small and medium-sized companies, some department stores employ the "retail" and "last in, first out" methods of identifying items, using Bureau of Labor Statistics Price Index for valuing closing inventory. In such an instance, the auditor would verify the use of the proper Index.

If the client uses a perpetual inventory method, the audit procedures would be modified in the following respects:

Extensive checks would be made from the inventory records to the physical stock. If results indicate that this area is satisfactory, a check would then be made from the physical stock back to the perpetual records. He would verify approximately the same dollar value that he would expect to verify if he were testing and observing a physical count. If tests indicate that the perpetual record is not accurate, it may be necessary for the auditor to suggest that an actual physical count be made of the entire inventory or of those sections of the inventory which the tests indicate are not sufficiently accurate to be reliable.

FINANCIAL STATEMENT PRESENTATION

Consistency in method of inventory valuation is of prime importance. If there has been any change in method of valuing the inventory since the last audit date, a complete explanation must be made, and the effect upon the current profit and loss statement must be stated. If the inventory, or a part of it is priced at the lower of cost or market, any material write-down to market must be explained and the effect upon the profit and loss statement stated. Also, if there has been a significant rise in market price above cost, this amount should be disclosed.

The basis of valuation should always be stated upon the balance sheet, if space permits, or explained in "Notes to Financial Statements" if a condensed figure must be used on the balance sheet. For example:

(*Under "Current Assets"*)

Inventories: (On a basis of first in, first out)

Raw Material—at lower of cost or market	$50,000	
Material in Process—at cost	25,000	
Finished Goods—at cost	75,000	$150,000

Space limitations may make it preferable to show the above as follows:

Inventories—Note A $150,000

Note A: Raw material is valued at the lower of cost or market, on a "first in, first out" basis. At the balance sheet date, the inventory was reduced by $5,000 to current market value; had this reduction not been made, net profit before income taxes would have been increased by $5,000. Material in process and finished goods are valued at cost, based upon the company's cost system, consistently used over the past five years, which appears to be reasonable.

In the "Supplemental Information" portion of the report, a comparative summary of the inventories should be made. Since the method of verifying the inventory is of importance to a credit grantor (that is, was an actual count made, if so when, if not what method was used?), it is advisable to include a very brief statement as to the procedure followed in obtaining the inventory valuations. The following might be considered a minimum for a manufacturing concern:

On September 30, 19xx employees of the corporation made a physical count of all material in process and of finished goods on hand, at which time our representatives were present and made extensive tests of the count and description of the items. Raw material is maintained on a perpetual record basis, and we satisfied ourselves that the inventory records were substantially correct.

All inventories are valued on a "first in, first out" basis. Raw material inventory is stated at cost which, at the balance sheet date was approximately $5,000 less than the cost of replacement. Material in process and finished goods are valued at manufactured cost, in conformity with the method used in prior years. A comparison with selling prices indicates that the finished goods inventory cost should permit a normal profit after allowing for ordinary selling and general and administrative expenses.

Damaged material, slow moving and obsolete items are stated at estimated net realizable values after allowing for sales and administrative expenses.

Following is a comparative summary of inventories for the years ended September 30, 19xx and 19xy:

	Year Ended September 30,	
	19xx	*19xy*
Raw material	$ 50,000	$ 65,000
Material in process	25,000	20,000
Finished goods	75,000	100,000
Total	$150,000	$185,000

7

Auditing Prepaid Expenses
and Other Assets

This chapter treats prepaid expenses and assets not represented in any other category. Every business organization carries insurance and, therefore, has unexpired premiums at the balance sheet date. In addition, most businesses have guaranty deposits for utilities, rent, telephone, and similar expenses. In addition to property and casualty insurance, life insurance is often carried on lives of officers and key employees on which the company is the beneficiary. If the life insurance is of the type that has a cash value, the cash value would be carried as "Other Assets." In addition, advances are often made to officers and employees for various reasons, and these are included in "Other Assets."

Under Internal Revenue Code provisions, cost of organization and reorganization costs cannot be expensed in the year incurred. They may, at the taxpayer's option, be amortized over a period not less than five years. In auditing a relatively new business, therefore, unamortized organization expense may be found.

Another example of deferred expense is advertising. The cost of an extensive campaign, including agency fees, media, printing, mailing, etc., may be deferred over the expected life of the program, rather than written off as expenditures are made. Similarly, the cost of a catalog, which could be quite large, might be written off over the expected life of the catalog, perhaps as long as two or three years. Such prepaid and deferred expenses are proper assets, but must be clearly identified as to their nature.

Somewhat less common in small organizations, are unamortized covenants not to compete (which usually arise out of the purchase of part or all of a going business), patents and trademarks, deferred research and development expense, and goodwill. As explained in Chapter 5, "Auditing Receivables," nontrade receivables are usually carried on the balance sheet as "Other Assets."

AUDIT PROGRAM

Subsequent to Audit Date

1. Prepare a trial balance of insurance policies having unexpired premiums at the balance sheet date.

2. Prepare trial balance of all life insurance policies under which the company is beneficiary.

3. Prepare trial balance for each general ledger account for all other deposits, prepaid expenses, etc.

4. Mail requests for confirmation of such assets as may be determined to require direct confirmation.

5. Make any necessary adjustments and post to working trial balance.

WORKING PAPERS REQUIRED

Unexpired Insurance

The trial balance for unexpired insurance should show the following:

- Number of policy.
- Insurer.
- Amount of coverage.
- Risk.
- Property insured.
- Total premium.
- Date of policy.
- Expiration date.
- Amount of premium unexpired at the audit date.

Pages 96 and 97 show a satisfactory form.

Fire and windstorm insurance is commonly written on a three- or five-year life. However, at the present time it is usual for smaller companies to finance a three- or five-year policy on a basis of paying slightly more than one year's premium in each of the earlier years. Since this can be financed at a very low rate of interest, it conserves working capital and accordingly is often used where cash may be limited. Where only one year's premium or a very little more is paid in one year, the remaining unexpired amount of insurance may be considered to be a current asset, since it will obviate the payment of cash within the ensuing 12-month period.

Comprehensive liability insurance, including automobile and truck insurance, workmen's compensation, and similar types of coverage, is usually written on a single-year basis. If this is the case, then definitely, any unexpired portion would constitute a current asset. On the going business concept, the unexpired premium is computed on a strictly pro rata basis rather than on a short-term cancellation basis, unless it is known that the policy will be cancelled by the policyholder. In this latter instance, the unexpired portion should be computed on the short-term cancellation basis.

The auditor should not be too concerned with minor differences in amounts of the unexpired portion, and should not make adjustments unless they are significant.

This is an area in which the auditor may wish to suggest to the client the value of a survey of his insurance coverage:

> In this field of insurance coverage, the CPA can be of significant value to his smaller clients. Only the CPA can be completely objective, since his income in no way depends upon whether or not the client buys insurance, and only the CPA has the complete knowledge necessary for a satisfactory insurance survey.[1]

Cash Value Life Insurance

A work sheet should be prepared showing for each policy the number, insurer, insured, beneficiary, annual premium, and cash value at audit date.

Deposits

A work sheet will be required for each general ledger account for deposits, showing for each the name of the person or company with whom the deposit is made, date of the deposit, date the deposit is due to be returned, and the amount of the deposit.

Many deposits will have an indefinite date of return. For example, most utility deposits will not be returned until service is discontinued. In this situation, the deposit is obviously not a current asset. On the other hand, deposits are often made on the purchase of equipment, for bids on contracts, deposits on rented equipment, etc., in which case there will be a definite termination date. The nature of the deposit and the date on which it is due to be returned will determine whether or not it constitutes a current or noncurrent asset.

Prepaid Expenses

For each general ledger account, a work sheet should be prepared, showing the date paid, amounts debited to the account, the amount written off during the current year, if any, name of the payee or other source of the entry, and the method of amortization.

Note: *Often there will be only one or two entries for each general ledger account, and if so, several accounts can be placed upon the same work sheet for convenience, or work sheets from the prior year's audit file can be transferred to the current year's file.*

---

[1] Frank Perry Walker, "A Casualty Insurance Survey for the Smaller Client," *Journal of Accountancy,* July, 1965, pp. 30–33.

XYZ Corporation
Unexpired Insurance
9-30-19XX

	COMPANY	AGENT	POLICY NUMBER	PROPERTY INSURED		RISK
	Acme Insurance Co.	Smith	1234567	Office Building		Fire + Extended Coverage
	" " "	"	4991111	Office Contents		Fire + Extended Coverage
	Casualty Insurance Co.	Jones	4114	Vehicles, Premises, Operations		General Comprehensive Liability
	" " "	"	X4332	Employees		Comprehensive Crime
	TOTAL					

Figure 7-1

AMOUNT OF POLICY	DATES		REMARKS				TOTAL PREMIUM	UNEXPIRED PREMIUM
	POLICY	EXPIRES						
300000	10-1-XY	10-1-XX	80% CO-INSURANCE				100000	50000
4000	6-8-XZ	6-8-XX					30000	5000
100/300	12-1-XY	12-1-XZ	NO PRODUCT LIABILITY				250000	100000
5000000	7-7-XY	7-7-XZ	OFFICERS EXCLUDED				90000	25000
								180000

Figure 7-1 (contd.)

Advances to Officers

An analysis should be made of all advances to officers, showing the date made, officer to whom made, amount, and the date when repayment is to be made.

Advances to Employees

A trial balance should be made for all advances to employees, showing the date made, name of employee, the amount, when repayment was made (subsequent to the audit date) or when repayment is to be paid, and reason for advance if other than a temporary payroll advance.

Organization Expense

Prepare a work sheet showing an analysis of the general ledger account.

Note: *On other than a first audit, the work sheet for the previous year can be transferred to the current file, and merely brought up to date. Current year's transactions normally will reflect only the write-off for the current year.*

Goodwill

A work sheet will be necessary, showing an analysis of the general ledger account.

Note: *Unless there are changes, the work sheet from the previous year's audit can be transferred to the current file.*

Patents and Trademarks

An analysis will be required for each general ledger account in this category.

Note: *Usually it is practicable to transfer the working papers for this account from the previous year's audit file.*

Covenant not to Compete

A work sheet will be required, showing the balance forward from the previous year, together with an analysis of all transactions for the current year.

Deferred Research and Development Expenses

Prepare a work sheet showing for each general ledger account the balance forward in the account together with an analysis of all transactions during the year.

Others

A work sheet should be prepared for any other asset account, not detailed above, showing for each the nature of the account and analysis of transactions for the year.

METHOD OF VERIFICATION

Unexpired Insurance

Unexpired premiums are normally verified by inspecting the policies themselves and determining that the unearned or unexpired premium has been properly computed. However, the auditor should check correspondence to determine that there has not been a cancellation. In the event that any question arises, it is a simple matter to verify directly with the agent representing the insurer that the policies are in force. This would ordinarily be done by letter. The amounts paid as premiums for the year may be verified by reference to the invoices from the agency or insurance company and to cancelled checks. It will usually be found that if mortgages are in effect, the originals of the insurance policies are delivered to the mortgagee, and the client has only memorandum copies of the insurance policies. In this case, the auditor should confirm directly with the holder, that the policies are the same as the memorandum copies and that they are in full effect.

Cash Value of Life Insurance

The amount of the cash value of the life insurance, under which the company is a beneficiary, should be confirmed directly by letter with the insurance carrier. At the same time, it is advisable to confirm that the corporation is indeed the beneficiary and to verify whether or not proceeds of the policy have been assigned. Following is a form of letter often used:

Life Insurance Company
New York, N. Y.

Gentlemen:

Subject: Policies:

#1234—John Doe, Insured

5678—Richard Roe, Insured

9101—John Smith, Insured

In connection with our regular audit, will you please confirm directly to our auditors, Able, Baker, and Carr, 1000 Central Avenue, Our Town, State, the following information with regard to each of the subject policies as of September 30, 19xx:

1. Beneficiary.
2. Amount of insurance.
3. Cash value.
4. Date to which premiums have been paid.
5. Assignment, if any, of proceeds and/or cash value.

A postage prepaid envelope is enclosed for your convenience.

Very truly yours,

XYZ Company

By _____
                          Treasurer

Deposits

Deposits which are not significant in amount, for example a $50 deposit on a utility account, substantiated by an invoice or cancelled check, need not normally be further verified. On the other hand, deposits of any material size, or any deposits of an unusual nature, or any deposits which on the audit date should have been returned, must be verified by direct correspondence with the holder.

Prepaid Expenses

Prepaid expenses are normally verified by reference to invoices and other vouchers supporting the charges made to the account. Due care should be exercised to determine that the charges are properly deferred. Whenever an organization experiences difficulty in generating enough cash to meet current expenses, there is always a tendency to defer expense in order to present a more favorable financial statement. While many expenses are properly deferred, and in some cases must be deferred for federal income tax purposes, the auditor cannot approve the inclusion of any deferred expenses which are not in accordance with generally accepted accounting principles.

Advances to Officers

This is a most important area, since advances to officers may have serious federal income tax implications. It is necessary first to determine from such information as is available, the reason for the advance. If it is in the nature of a semipermanent loan, the Internal Revenue Service is likely to consider this to be a dividend if the officer is a stockholder. In any event there very definitely should be authorization by the board of directors, which would be duly entered in the minutes. If a note has been secured from the officer the note should be inspected, and if the amount is material it should be confirmed directly with the officer. If interest is to be paid, any amount due and unpaid at the audit date should be accrued. In this connection, it should be remembered that any accrual to a related cash basis taxpayer not paid within two and one-half months from the end of the taxable year, will be disallowed as a tax deduction.

It is common practice to make advances to officers for travel and other anticipated expenses, which the officer will pay on behalf of the corporation. In some small organizations, it is often difficult for the bookkeeper to prevail upon the officer to make up a proper travel or other expense report, which will clear the advance. The auditor can be of real service to his client in this area by calling to his attention the requirements of the Internal Revenue Service in regard to reimbursed expenses, and the tax consequences, particularly to the individual, of failure to properly comply with the regulations.

Advances to Employees

It is rather common in larger organizations for the company to make temporary advances to its employees, particularly those in the lower pay brackets. If this practice is allowed to become extensive it can be quite costly in bookkeeping time for the client, and the auditor should point this out to the client if such is found to be the case.

Ordinary payroll advances can be fairly easily verified by tracing the repayment of the deduction to a subsequent pay period. Usually an amount advanced will be deducted in a reasonably short time, so that the auditor will be able to verify the repayment of funds from the available bookkeeping data.

Travel and other expense advances are also made to employees who are not officers, but proper travel expense reports can more easily be obtained from these employees, and accordingly are usually cleared promptly. Verification is made by reference to expense reports filed subsequent to the audit date.

Organization Expense

An item commonly found with newer corporations will be unamortized organization expense. Internal Revenue Code, section 248, grants a corporation an election to treat its expenditures for organization as deferred expenses, which can be deducted over a period of 60 months or more, at the option of the corporation. The election applies to organization expenditures incurred after August 16, 1954. It is important to note that if the amortization is to be taken for tax purposes, that the election be made the first year. Verification of organization expenses is normally made by reference to the applicable expenditures, usually consisting of legal fees, fees paid to a state for registration, and similar items. It is important to note which expenditures are allowable as organization expense. Most expenditures involved in organizing a corporation are organization expense, the chief exception being any commissions or expenses in selling and issuing capital stock of a corporation. However, since small and medium-sized companies rarely have a public stock issue, this question does not often arise in auditing companies of this size.

Goodwill

According to accounting theory, goodwill in its simplest form is the excess paid for an asset over its book value, the excess representing future benefits to be received by the purchaser. To verify the amount carried as goodwill on the client's books, the auditor will look to the agreement under which the goodwill was acquired. If buyer and seller are agreed upon the allocation, and the amount is reasonable, the Internal Revenue Service will not usually upset the allocation. The value of goodwill thus arrived at will ordinarily be the amount carried on the books. Any subsequent charges or credits to the account would be verified by reference to the transaction. The auditor has the responsibility of determining that all entries to the account are proper. Goodwill is considered to be a capital asset and cannot be amortized for income tax purposes.

Patents, Copyrights, and Trademarks

Capitalized patents and copyrights are not often encountered in small businesses, but when they do appear amounts would be verified by checking against invoices and other evidence of expenditures, such as payroll records, cash payments, etc. Patents and copyrights are depreciable over their useful life, which generally is 17 years for patents and 28 years for copyrights. However, other lives may be used under certain circumstances.

Trademark and trade names can, if desired, be amortized over a period of not less than 60 months, under Code section 177 (b). However, it should be noted that the amortization of this expense does not extend to the consideration paid for the purchase of any existing trade name, trademark, or business, which are properly capitalizable.

Research and Experimental Expenses

Research and experimental expenses, if encountered, can be treated in one of two ways, as deductible expenses or capitalized. If the company has elected to capitalize such expenditures under IRS Code, section 174 they may be written off over a period of not less than 60 months, beginning with the month in which benefits are first realized.

In this respect, it is noted that the expenditures must be in connection with the regular trade or business. If such an account appears, it would be necessary to verify the charges to the account for the year and determine that they are actual research and experimental expenditures. Verification would depend upon the source of the charges, which might be from outside agencies, in which case invoices and other pertinent data would be examined, or it may arise from internal distribution, such as payroll expenditures, supplies, etc., all of which can be verified in the usual manner.

REQUIREMENTS OF SPECIAL SITUATIONS

Under certain circumstances, there may be an understandable tendency on the part of management to attempt to increase reported profit or decrease reported loss by deferring expenditures rather than expensing them currently. This becomes particularly apparent in the category of deferred expenses, since by definition these are truly expenses, which are deferred for the purpose of relating income to expense in any particular period. The auditor must be extremely careful to determine that these deferred expenses are indeed properly attributable to some future period of time rather than to the period being audited.

For inclusion in the area of deferred expenses, there must be a demonstrable benefit to the business in the future to permit the inclusion of the deferred expense as an asset. For example, prepaid insurance policies can definitely be shown to have a value to future operations. On the other hand, it may be difficult to show that there will be any benefit to future operations of deferred research and development expenses if no new product has actually emerged from this activity.

An unfortunate situation may arise in the event that the client is forced into receivership or liquidation. Under these circumstances, prepaid and deferred expenses often have no liquidating value. If they have constituted a material portion of the assets, the trustee may criticize the auditor for including them as assets in the earlier financial statements, and may even go so far as to attempt to force the auditor to reimburse the estate for the amount of the improper deferred assets.

FINANCIAL STATEMENT PRESENTATION

Working papers will indicate which items are current and which are not current assets. There is not unanimous agreement that prepaid insurance and other prepaid items should be carried as a current asset, even though they will obviate the use of cash during the ensuing 12 months, which conforms to the general definition of a current asset. However, as applying to smaller businesses, unexpired insurance, provided the unexpired portion is for no more than 12 months from the balance sheet date, is usually shown as a current asset.

On the other hand, deposits which have no definite date of repayment must be treated as noncurrent assets. In the event that a company does have patents, trademarks, capitalized research and development expense, and items of a similar nature, they would be shown as noncurrent assets. Contracts, leases, and other intangible assets which do not have a present capitalizable value may be mentioned in footnotes. Balance sheet presentation would be as follows:

Other assets (noncurrent):

Unamortized organization expense	$ 500.00
Unamortized portion of covenant not to compete	3,000.00
Cash value—life insurance	5,000.00
Total	$8,500.00

In the event that any of the assets had been pledged, they would be so noted with a suitable note in the "Notes to Financial Statements." Following is one way in which this may be shown:

Note A: The company has pledged the cash value of life insurance on officers of the corporation, of which the company is beneficiary, to the Blank National Bank as additional security for notes due in the principal amount of $500,000, repayment of which is due at the rate of $1,000 per month.

If a company has elected to expense experimental and development expense rather than to capitalize and amortize, and if the amount is material, a notation should be made in "Notes to Financial Statements," following this general outline:

Note B: During the year, the corporation expended the sum of $500,000 on experimental and development expenses which it has elected to expense rather than capitalize.

Auditing Fixed
Assets

The importance of fixed assets as a total of the assets of the enterprise varies quite materially with the type of business. For a wholesale establishment, for example, fixed assets usually constitute a rather small part of the company's total assets. On the other hand, for a utility, fixed assets may be by far the most significant asset on the balance sheet.

The auditor of a small enterprise has a considerable advantage in that he can easily become familiar with the major items of equipment, furniture, and fixtures. It is always advisable to actually view major additions for the year, and this can be done conveniently at the time the observation of the inventory count is made. Accordingly, prior to the audit date the auditor should review the general ledger for major additions to fixed assets as well as any retirements which may have been made, and be alert for observing the additions during the time that he is verifying the inventory.

In some instances, it is common practice for a client to manufacture, install, or assemble equipment. Such costs are properly capitalizable, and, in fact, must be capitalized for the purpose of federal income tax computation. It is important that the client be aware of the fact that in order to properly capitalize these expenditures, adequate detail records must be maintained. Ideally, a work order would be issued for the labor and material to be used for the assembly and installation of equipment, and all charges would be made to this work order. Unfortunately, most smaller-sized businesses do not follow this procedure, so that the auditor is often forced to dig through company records to verify the correct cost of installation. In this connection petty cash must not be overlooked, since often minor disbursements are paid by cash.

There are, of course, a number of ways in which the client may keep a record of fixed assets. In the writer's opinion, the most satisfactory method is a detailed fixed asset ledger, with each capitalizable asset being given a page. This may be done even though reporting for federal income taxes is made under Revenue Procedures 62-21 and 65-13.

Occasionally a major creditor, such as a bank, may request a list of the significant property items. A detailed fixed asset record facilitates the preparation of such a report. In addition, by including model number, serial number, and other detailed information pertaining to equipment, the ordering of parts is expedited. If the 20 per cent "bonus depreciation" is taken, it is essential that a detail record be maintained. Likewise investment credit must be noted. The most convenient place to do this is in the detailed asset ledger.

Another reason for maintaining detailed records is that many assets, particularly automobiles, trucks, and office machines have a tendency to be traded rather frequently. Without a detailed record it is very difficult to compute the accumulated depreciation, relieve the allowance for depreciation account and the asset account, and compute taxable gain or loss. This latter takes on added significance with the application of IRC Sections 1245 and 1250 which require a breakdown of depreciation taken during specific periods. Liability for recapture of investment credit is easily determined by reference to a properly maintained detail fixed asset record.

The question frequently arises as to the proper determination of what constitutes a capital asset. This may be particularly troublesome in the area of perishable tools, such as fractional horsepower electric drills, gauges, small hand tools, and the like. These constitute a somewhat doubtful fixed asset, since it is seldom practicable to inventory them and management rarely has knowledge of the actual value on hand at the balance sheet date. Accordingly, the most conservative approach is to expense them as they are purchased.

An alternative, often encountered, is to find a figure in the general ledger valuing perishable tools at a flat amount, which represents an average inventory. Subsequent purchases are expensed, on the basic principle that such additional purchases merely replace tools previously included and do not add to the total asset value. It is necessary on a first audit that the auditor satisfy himself by means of actual observation, reference to invoices, and discussion with company officials, that the value of perishable tools stated on the books is a reasonable figure.

Another area of question will arise among such things as dies, patterns, molds, and similar items. In each case it will be necessary to determine the average life of the items, and if they have a reasonable life expectation of more than one year they should be capitalized and depreciated over their estimated useful life. In the case of small corporations especially, it is quite desirable to have the book basis and the tax basis be the same to avoid the lengthy and time-consuming process of preparing two sets of statements. However, tax treatment does not always conform to good accounting practice, and good accounting practice should never be sacrificed to tax expediency.

In recent years, it has become very common for business enterprises to lease buildings and equipment which earlier it was more customary to purchase. The Accounting Principles Board of the American Institute of Certified Public Accountants has issued an opinion of the reporting of leases in financial statements of lessors.[1]

This opinion took cognizance of the fact that some leases are, for all practical purposes noncancellable, provide for ultimate purchase, and take on the aspects of a purchase on installments. Assets covered by such a lease should be treated as assets owned, with the accompanying liability shown on the balance sheet. In the case of all leases, except those for relatively short periods which do not provide for any ultimate purchase by lessor, all of the circumstances surrounding the lease, its terms, provision for cancellation, etc. must be carefully scrutinized to determine whether the lease is to be treated as a lease or as a purchase on deferred terms.

As to the application to federal income tax returns, the intention of the parties will normally control, but there have been instances where unusual terms in the lease agreement have led the Internal Revenue Service to rule that a lease was not a lease but an installment sale.[2]

In accordance with the opinion cited above, whenever leases are material in amount, the report should disclose either in the report itself or as footnotes to the financial statements, the pertinent information, including among other things the annual rental amount, terms of the lease, and a general description of the assets involved.

AUDIT PROGRAM

Prior to the Audit Date

1. Examine the general ledger for major additions and retirements, so that they can be observed during the check of the inventory count.

Subsequent to Audit Date

1. Prepare an analysis of each general ledger fixed asset account and allowance for depreciation account.

2. Verify each significant addition by examining vendors' invoices, freight bills, work orders if installation or fabrication is performed in client's plant, and any other data applicable. In examining vendors' invoices, terms should be noted carefully, particularly as to whether or not freight is included, and whether or not additional expense for local cartage, installation, etc. will be required. When machinery is shipped FOB, vendor's plant freight is often overlooked. Terms of payment should also be noted. If payment is to be deferred by means of installment payments, the liability should be traced to payables.

---

[1] "Accounting for Leases in Financial Statements of Lessors," Opinions of the Accounting Principles Board #7, American Institute of Certified Public Accountants, New York.

[2] *Benton v. Comm.* 197 F 2d 745, AFTR 229; *Judson Mills* 11 T.C. 25, *Holeproof Hosiery Co.* 11 BTA 547.

3. Major items of equipment added during the year under review should actually be observed in place.

4. An adding machine tape of the detail asset ledger should be made to determine that the detail is in agreement with the general ledger controlling account. A similar adding machine tape should be made of the accumulated depreciation at the audit date.

5. Test the amount of depreciation for each new addition for the year and determine that the life used and the method of depreciation used is proper.

6. Verify the retirement of each asset during the year by reference to sales invoices, if the item has been sold, and to work orders or similar vouchers if the item has been scrapped. In the event of a major retirement, such as the razing of a building, the area should be inspected.

7. Minutes of the board of director's meetings should be scrutinized for authorization for the purchase of new assets and for the retirement of old assets. In some jurisdictions approval for the purchase of major new assets, and more commonly, approval for the sale of assets must be made by stockholders, so that reference to minutes of stockholders' meetings is necessary.

8. Prepare and post to working trial balance any necessary adjusting journal entries.

WORKING PAPERS REQUIRED

Permanent File

1. *Land:* On the occasion of first audit, and when subsequent land acquisitions are made, a thorough examination of all applicable papers must be made. These will probably include, as a minimum, the following:

   Authorization: *Minutes of stockholders' meetings, if such action is required; minutes of board of directors' meetings.*

   Purchase: *Purchase is usually evidenced by a deed, the exact form varying with the jurisdiction; in addition, there will be attorneys' opinions, escrow statements, title insurance, and other instruments, depending again upon the jurisdiction and the circumstances. The auditor is entitled to rely upon the opinion of attorneys as to legal title. As a precaution, however, the auditor should independently verify that title lies with the client as recorded with the appropriate public official.*

   Note: *Considerable time can be saved, and the file will be more complete, if actual copies of the various instruments can be made and put into the file. A summary of costs should be prepared and placed with above copies and/or abstracts.*

2. *Buildings:* A similar file should be maintained for buildings, land improvements such as water and sewer lines, wells, switch tracks, pavements, etc. If desired, land improvements can be maintained in the land file. If an asset is constructed, all of the appropriate detail including contracts and subcontracts, labor and material furnished by the client, and any other costs must be detailed. Since, in most cases, this material is quite voluminous, it is usually not practicable to keep complete copies in the auditor's file; therefore, summaries can be made and kept in the auditor's file.

Current Audit File

Opinion 12 of the Accounting Principles Board of the American Institute of Certified Public Accountants states, regarding depreciable assets and depreciation, that:

> Because of the significant effects on financial position and results of operations of the depreciation method or methods used, the following disclosures should be made in the financial statements or in notes thereto:
>
> a. Depreciation for the period.
> b. Balances of major classes of depreciable assets, by nature or function, at the balance sheet date.
> c. Accumulated depreciation, either by major classes of depreciable assets or in total at the balance sheet date.
> d. A general description of the method or methods used in computing depreciation with respect to major classes of depreciable assets.[3]

Preparation of work papers in accordance with the following will provide the necessary information to comply adequately with the foregoing opinion.

Assets: *Prepare one work sheet for each general ledger account, showing the balance forward at the beginning of the year, which must agree with previous year's closing balance; list each addition showing vendor, date of purchase and installation, cost, and journal reference. Retirements should be listed in the same manner. Footings should be proved and compared with the balance in the general ledger.*

Page 110 shows an example of the general ledger account work sheet.

Note: *Some auditors prefer to transfer the general ledger fixed asset work sheets from the prior audit file to the current year's audit file. This procedure has the advantage of avoiding the necessity of preparing new work sheets each year as well as verifying the opening balances. This method is satisfactory if the number of additions and retirements is relatively small.*

From the information shown on the work sheet illustrated in Figure 8-1, a summary can be prepared showing all of the information necessary for the preparation of the "Computation of Investment Credit" for the federal income tax return, as well as the recapture of the investment credit, if such is involved. Page 111 shows a satisfactory form of the investment credit summary.

Allowance for Depreciation

A work sheet should be prepared for each general ledger account for allowance for depreciation. This work sheet should show the opening balance, retirements, and

---

[3] "Opinions of the Accounting Principles Board #12," American Institute of Certified Public Accountants, New York.

XYZ Corporation
Office Equipment - Ac #210
9-30-19XX

						REF.		DR.		CR.		BAL.	
BAL.	10-1-19XX											1500000	
11-15	ACCTG. MACHINE NEW - 10YR. LIFE					PJ	11-2	800000				2300000	
12-1	SOLD ACCTG. MACHINE PUR. 7-15-XZ ORIG. 10YR. LIFE - USED 6YRS. - INVESTMENT CREDIT TAKEN: 140.00					CR	12-1			200000		2100000	
4-19	OFFSET PRESS USED 10YR. LIFE					PJ	4-1	200000				2300000	

Figure 8-1

XYZ Corporation
Summary - Investment - Credit
9 - 30 - 19XX

	Total	Less Than 4	4 to 6	6 to 8	8 or More
Production Machinery					
New	3450000	450000	300000	200000	2500000
Used	550000	100000	300000	150000	
Total	4000000	550000	600000	350000	2500000
Office Equipment					
New	800000				800000
Used	200000			200000	
Total	1000000			200000	800000
Summary					
New	4250000	450000	300000	200000	3300000
Used	750000	100000	300000	350000	
Total	5000000	550000	600000	550000	3300000
Recapture:					
Acctg. Machine: Cost		200000			
10 yr. Life					
Used:	6 Years				
	Declining Balance				
	Depreciation Claimed:	150000			

Figure 8-2

the provision for the current year's depreciation. If this latter consists of 12 equal monthly entries—a very common procedure—they can be totalled and one entry made. This is illustrated in Figure 8-3.

> **Note:** *This is usually the most convenient point at which to summarize the amount of depreciation charged each year by the various methods of depreciation, including the 20 per cent "bonus depreciation."*

Summary of Depreciation

From the allowance for depreciation general ledger account work sheets a summary of depreciation can be prepared, which provides all of the information necessary for statements and for federal income tax returns. Page 114 shows an example.

METHOD OF VERIFICATION

Assets

All additions to fixed assets are verified by comparing data on the work sheet with vendors' invoices, work orders, or other documents. Retirements are verified in a like manner.

Accumulated Depreciation

Current year's provision is verified by comparison with the detail adding machine tape, obtained by adding the year's provision as shown on the detail fixed asset ledger.

> **Note:** *The above procedure is based upon the client's maintaining some type of detail fixed asset records, where date and cost of acquisition, life, method of depreciation, and accumulated depreciation is available. Some businesses will be found to keep only very sketchy records, often grouped by type of equipment, such as "trucks" or "office furniture," or even by location such as "Central Avenue store" or "factory office." In such cases it will be necessary to analyze each group on the occasion of a first audit, to verify the cost and rate, method, and amount of depreciation. Subsequent additions and retirements can be audited in the same manner as for businesses maintaining a detail asset ledger. In view of the advantages of a detail record system, however, particularly with regard to income tax returns, the client is well advised to keep adequate records.*

REQUIREMENTS OF SPECIAL SITUATIONS

When businesses face a chronic working capital shortage, there is some tendency to capitalize rather than expense any borderline purchase. This usually causes the auditor little trouble, since he will find it in the fixed asset accounts and will routinely take appropriate action. Occasionally, however, the reverse becomes true as businesses

XYZ CORPORATION
ALLOW DEPRN. - OFFICE EQUIP. - AC #2100
9 - 30 - 19XX

		REF.	DR.	CR.	BAL.
BAL. 10-1-19XX					700000
PROVISION - YEAR (12 @ $375)		RJE		450000	
12-1 RETIRE ACCTG. MACH.		CR 12-1	150000		1000000
SUMMARY OF PROVISION:					
STRAIGHT LINE				150000	
DECLINING BALANCE				300000	
				450000	
NOTE: ALL 20% FIRST YEAR DEPRECIATION TAKEN ON MACHINERY - AC #250					

Figure 8-3

XYZ Corporation.
Summary of Depreciation 9-30-19XX

| | Accumulated Depreciation 10-1-19XY | Depreciation Provision | | | | | Retirements | Accumulated Depreciation 9-30-19XX |
		Straight Line	Declining Balance	Sum. of Digits	20% First Year	Total Provision		
Buildings	3500000	250000		500000		750000		4250000
Production Machinery	4200000		1500000	300000	200000	2000000	1000000	5200000
Office Equipment	700000	150000	300000			450000	150000	1000000
Total	8400000	400000	1800000	800000	200000	3200000	1150000	10450000

Figure 8-4

generate substantial taxable income at high rates. This situation is somewhat more difficult to detect, because the expenses will be distributed over a large area. A careful analysis of the maintenance and repair accounts, which will be made in connection with the audit of income and expense accounts, should disclose any questionable items. A comparison of purchases of new or additional equipment between two or more fiscal years may also point out areas for further investigation.

FINANCIAL STATEMENT PRESENTATION

Balance sheet presentation will vary with the type of assets and with their significance, relative to the total assets. In the case of businesses with relatively small fixed assets, and if the method and amount of depreciation does not require special disclosure in accordance with Opinion 12, cited earlier, the following may be satisfactory:

Fixed Assets—At cost	$10,750	
Less: Allowance for Depreciation	2,500	
Net Book Value		$8,250

Note: *Several captions are in general use, the more common being "Plant, Property, and Equipment," "Plant Property," "Land and Depreciable Property," and "Fixed Assets."*

If the fixed assets of a company are a significant part of total assets, it may be desirable to show more detail on the balance sheet:

Plant, Property, and Equipment: at cost:		
Buildings	$150,000	
Machinery	350,000	
Office furniture and equipment	50,000	
	550,000	
Less: Allowance for depreciation	175,000	
	375,000	
Land	125,000	$500,000

The basis of valuing fixed assets on the books of the enterprise must always be stated. The most common basis is cost, and it may be so stated on the balance sheet as shown in the foregoing examples. The use of any other basis will usually require a longer explanation and can best be done in a "Note to Financial Statement." For example, if the company has issued capital stock for certain land and buildings, it can be explained as follows:

X Y Z CORPORATION

FIXED ASSETS AND DEPRECIATION
SEPTEMBER 30, 19xx

	Cost				Accumulated Depreciation			
	Balance October 1, 19xx	Additions	Retirements	Balance September 30, 19xx	Balance October 1, 19xx	Provision Fiscal Year	Retirements	Balance September 30, 19xx
Depreciable property:								
Buildings	$250,000	$	$	$250,000	$35,000	$ 7,500	$	$ 42,500
Production machinery	250,000	40,000	25,000	265,000	42,000	20,000	10,000	52,000
Office equipment	15,000	10,000	2,000	23,000	7,000	4,500	1,500	10,000
Total depreciable assets	515,000	50,000	27,000	538,000	$84,000	$32,000	$11,500	$104,500
Land	100,000			100,000				
	$615,000	$50,000	$27,000	$638,000				

Figure 8-5

Note A: The corporation issued capital stock with a stated value of $100,000 for five acres of land and a building presently used for an office and warehouse. This value was determined to be the fair market value at the time of the transaction as determined by an independent appraiser and approved by the board of directors.

In the past it was rather common for corporations to buy up various properties, have them reappraised at a much higher value, and then reflect the higher value on the books and in the financial statements. Such practice has now fallen into disrepute, and is seldom encountered by the auditor. When any basis is used, other than cost, the auditor must satisfy himself that the basis is one that conforms to generally accepted accounting principles.

The total amount of depreciation taken for the fiscal year must be shown. This will usually appear in the Income Account, but may also be shown in a "Note to Financial Statement." Following is an example of the latter, which also includes a statement in regard to the method of depreciation used:

Note A: Total depreciation charged against operations for the year amounted to $32,000. Of this amount, $2,000 represented first-year "bonus depreciation" and $26,000 represented accelerated depreciation allowed under current Internal Revenue Service regulations. Had straight-line depreciation been used for all depreciable assets, depreciation expense for the year would have been decreased by $10,000 and net income before income taxes would have been increased by a like amount.

In the Supplemental Information section of the report, a summary should be furnished showing the detail of the property accounts and the accumulated depreciation. Figure 8-5 shows a suggested form.

9

Auditing Notes
Payable

The term "Notes Payable" is generally understood to include notes, drafts, conditional sales contracts, mortgages, bonds, and similar instruments. Each may arise through the purchase of merchandise, the loan of money, the purchase of equipment, and other fixed assets and, in somewhat rare instances, even for the purchase of initial capital stock. The instrument securing the payment of a note will depend upon the jurisdiction in which the asset is located, and it is assumed that the auditor is familiar with the requirements of his particular state. One thing that is common to almost all is that the instrument be filed for record with one or more governmental agencies.

Organizations frequently borrow money by pledging certain assets of the corporation as security for the payment of a note. These assets may be personalty, which ordinarily is secured by a chattel mortgage (or equivalent) or realty, which is commonly secured by a trust indenture or mortgage. In certain cases, particularly for loans made by the Small Business Administration or guaranteed by that agency, a blanket chattel mortgage is given to cover all present chattels and chattels to be acquired in the future. Such liens, of course, are subject to any prior purchase money obligation until such has been paid in full.

Notes Payable will ordinarily fall into one of the following categories:

1. Notes payable—unsecured.
2. Notes payable—secured.
3. Drafts.

   Note: *This type of negotiable instrument was common in the past when merchandise was shipped on a term draft basis. Although presently used for shipments which must be paid before being released by the carrier, the use of drafts has become*

119

considerably less common. The drafts presently encountered in normal transactions of smaller businesses will usually be paid at sight, and thus will seldom appear on a balance sheet.

4. Conditional sales contract.

   Note: *This is used in certain jurisdictions in lieu of a note and chattel mortgage, and in effect title to merchandise remains with the vendor until the amount is paid in full. As a practical matter, conditional sales contracts are usually treated by the auditor in the same manner as notes secured by chattel mortgage, although there is a distinct legal difference.*

5. Bonds.

   Note: *It is somewhat rare for smaller corporations to issue bonds because of their relatively high cost. However, these will occasionally be found.*

As stated above, bonds are rather rarely issued by small businesses in the manufacturing or mercantile areas. However, they are frequently used to raise substantial capital by hospitals, businesses owning and operating commercial and industrial real estate, and other sectors of the business community. For those businesses which have bonds outstanding, the audit procedures will vary slightly from those applying to notes and mortgages payable.

Bonds are usually issued serially in various denominations, the most usual being $1,000. In the United States, the most common form of bond is a bearer bond with interest coupons attached. The coupons will show the amount of the interest due and the date due, bond interest most commonly being paid semiannually. Usually a bank or trust company is appointed as trustee for the bondholders and bonds are issued under its control. The company issuing the bonds makes deposits on the appropriate date to take care of the bond coupons which will be presented to the trustee for the interest payments. Also, many bond issues provide for a sinking fund which requires that the issuer deposit certain sums of money with the trustee for the purpose of redeeming bonds. Sometimes this may be a fixed amount, and other times it is determined by the amount of profit earned by the business. In addition, bonds may be required to be retired whenever fixed assets are sold.

Bonds may be either secured or unsecured. Unsecured bonds are usually referred to as "debentures." If bonds are to be secured, the security will be fully described in the trust indenture. Ordinarily, if any property which is used to secure the bond issue is sold, proceeds must be deposited with the trustee for the purpose of retiring bonds.

Bonds are often issued at a discount. Discount represents an additional price paid for the use of the money and is the equivalent of interest. The discount should be charged ratably over the life of the bond issue, and a charge should be made to operating expense each year of the amount of discount attributable to that year. This has the effect of charging each year with its share of the discount expense. It is usual to charge the bond discount expense to the interest expense account. At the time that the bonds are issued, the amount of the discount would be debited to a prepaid expense account.

Occasionally, bonds have been issued at a premium. The premium operates in a similar manner to discount except, of course, that it is in reverse. In other words, the amount represents a reduction in the cost of borrowing money and should be distributed ratably over the life of the bonds as a credit to interest expense. At the time that the bonds are sold, the premium would be set up in a reserve account usually captioned "Reserve for Bond Premium." However, in smaller businesses, if bonds are issued at all, they are more likely to be issued at a discount than at a premium.

Normally the bond and the interest coupons will have printed on them the place, usually a bank, where they may be presented for payment when due. The company issuing the bonds will, of course, prior to the due date of either principal or interest, deposit to a special account the funds necessary to make the payments due.

AUDIT PROGRAM

As of Audit Date

1. Prepare trial balance of notes payable, with separate trial balances for each category, if the volume justifies.
2. Compare detail ledger or other detail information with trial balance.

Subsequent to Audit Date

1. Mail request for confirmation to noteholder.
2. Mail request for confirmation to bond trustee.
3. Prove trial balance footings and extensions.
4. Compare returned confirmation requests, checking especially for security, if any, due dates, status of interest, and delinquencies, if any.
5. Follow up any confirmation requests not returned.
6. Resolve any discrepancies reported by noteholders; prepare and post to working trial balance any necessary adjusting journal entries.

WORKING PAPERS REQUIRED

Permanent File

The permanent file should contain a reference to the bylaws of the corporation to determine to what extent stockholders' approval is required for pledging assets of the corporation and for borrowing money. In many cases, this is governed not only by corporation bylaws but by statutory requirements as well. It is assumed that the auditor is familiar with the statutory requirements of his jurisdiction. It should be determined that all mortgages, bonds, and other major borrowings have received whatever approval is required by action of stockholders and/or board of directors.

The permanent file should contain references to the appropriate minutes, indicating approval for each such note. In the case of mortgages, it is desirable to keep a facsimile copy of the mortgage in the permanent file for convenient reference. Many companies keep carbon copies of their notes payable, and if so, it is convenient for the auditor to make copies for his own permanent file. Likewise, copies of any bond indentures, agreements, etc., should be put into the permanent file.

If the client has a real estate mortgage, on the occasion of the first audit this should be carefully scrutinized to determine that the property descriptions are correct and that the records in the books agree with such documents as may be filed for public record.

Current Audit File

If there are only a few notes payable, including conditional sales contracts, etc., only one trial balance would be required. If, however, there are numerous notes payable, a separate trial balance should be prepared for each general category. The trial balance of bonds outstanding should always be kept separate from other obligations.

The trial balance of notes payable should show the following information:

1. Payee.
2. Original amount of note.
3. Amount due at audit date.
4. Rate of interest.
5. Amount of interest accrued at audit date, if any.
6. Amount of interest prepaid at audit date, if any.
7. Principal amount due within one year.
8. Principal amount due after one year.
9. Security, if any.
10. Term of note.
11. Date of original note.
12. Date of approval of board of directors, and/or shareholders, if required.

The foregoing is prepared from the permanent file, the general ledger, and/or subsidiary ledgers. Figure 9-1 on pages 124 and 125 illustrates the trial balance.

Trial balance of bonds outstanding should show the following information (see also Figure 9-2 on pages 126 and 127).

Note: *Terms of the bond indenture will be in the permanent file, and since all bonds with the same maturity date may be grouped together, list the serial numbers as shown in the illustration below.*

1. Date of original issue.
2. Serial number or numbers of bonds.
3. Due date of bonds.
4. Interest accrued to audit date.
5. Amount due within one year.
6. Amount due after one year.
7. Interest rate.
8. Type of bond and/or security.

METHOD OF VERIFICATION

The only satisfactory method of verifying notes payable is by direct correspondence with the holders thereof. The request for confirmation should be made in letter form and should be signed by a responsible officer of the client. A mere request by the auditor for such confirmation without the written approval of an officer of the client will frequently result in the confirmation being ignored, since the auditor individually has no right to this information without the written approval of the client.

The confirmation should request that the holder confirm directly to the auditor the amount owing at the balance sheet date; the amount of prepaid interest, if any; the amount of accrued interest, if any; rate of interest; security, if any; and whether or not any default exists at the time of the confirmation. Request for confirmation should be mailed as closely as possible to the audit date, to allow time for follow-up, if necessary. The exact form of the confirmation is not critical. Many auditors have a standard printed form; others use a letter, usually prepared by the client on the client's stationery. Following is a letter form often used:

FGH Corporation
Industrial Avenue
Our Town, State

Gentlemen:

Our auditors, Able, Baker, and Carr, 1000 Central Avenue, Our Town, State, are making their usual examination of our books and records, as of September 30, 19xx. Will you please confirm directly to them the following information, as of September 30, 19xx, in regard to our note which you hold:

           Amount owing at September 30, 19xx $_____

           Amount past due, if any $_____

           Amount of interest due, if any $_____

           Amount of prepaid interest, if any $_____

           Security, if any _____

           Due date of note   _____

A postage prepaid envelope, addressed to our auditors, is enclosed for your convenience.

                    Very truly yours,

                    XYZ Company

                    By _____
                                    Treasurer

XYZ COMPANY
NOTES PAYABLE
9-30-19XX

PAYEE	AMOUNT		RATE OF INTEREST	ACCRUED INTEREST 9-30-XX	PREPAID INTEREST 9-30-XX
	ORIGINAL	DUE 9-30-XX			
FIRST NATIONAL BANK	1000000	1000000	8%	13333	—
A AUTO COMPANY	600000	480000	INCLUDED	—	24000
I INSURANCE COMPANY	10000000	10000000	6%	25000	—
M MANUFACTURING, INC.	500000	400000	6%	—	—
TOTAL		11880000		38333	24000

Figure 9-1

PRINCIPAL DUE		SECURITY			TERM OF NOTE		DATE OF NOTE	APPROVAL
WITHIN 1 YEAR	AFTER 1 YEAR							
1000000	—	NONE			90	DA.	7-1-XX	6-30-XX
240000	240000	19XX FORD TRUCK – ONE TON			30	MO.	4-1-XX	3-15-XX
—	10000000	LAND AND BUILDINGS			15	YRS.	3-15-YY	2-10-YY
100000	300000	FORK LIFT TRUCK			5	YRS.	10-1-YY	9-10-YY
1340000	10540000							

Figure 9-1 (contd.)

XYZ Company
Bonds Payable
9-30-19XX

| DATE ISSUED | SERIAL NUMBERS | | DUE DATE | INTEREST ACCRUED TO 9-30-XX | AMOUNT WITHIN 1 YEAR |
	FROM	TO (INCLUSIVE)			
10-1-19YY	1	25	10-1-YZ	75000	-
10-1-19YZ	26	50	10-1-ZZ	75000	-
10-1-19AA	51	75	10-1-BB	62500	-
10-1-19AB	76	100	10-1-BC	62500	-
TOTAL				275000	

Figure 9-2

DUE AFTER 1 YEAR	INTEREST RATE	NOTE:							
2500000	6%	DEBENTURES - 20 YEARS							
2500000	6%	" " "							
2500000	5%	FIRST MORTGAGE - 20 YEARS							
2500000	5%	" " " "							
10000000									

Figure 9-2 (contd.)

It is advisable to send request for confirmation to any creditor who appears on the books to be a noteholder continually throughout the year, but who at the audit date indicates no unpaid balance. It is also advisable to check available records at the appropriate governmental agency, usually a state or county recorder, for evidences of mortgages, liens, and other indebtedness, to determine if any obligation exists not recorded on the company's books.

Confirmation of bonds outstanding will normally be made by a request to the trustee of the bond indenture. The following information should be requested:

1. Total value of the bonds outstanding at the audit date.
2. Amount past due, if any.
3. Amount in sinking fund, if any.
4. Amount of interest due but unpaid.
5. Due dates of outstanding bonds at audit date.
6. Whether or not there are any violations of the trust indenture at the audit date.
7. Status of paid coupons.

> **Note:** *Coupons normally are cancelled by the trustee when paid, and often are burned, with a cremation certificate being issued. If the trustee is a bank or legally constituted trust company, it is usually sufficient to receive a letter showing the above information. If, however, the auditor has any questions as to the bonifides or the ability of the trustee to keep such records, he should personally examine any cancelled bonds which have been paid during the audit period and all cancelled interest coupons which have been paid during the audit period, to satisfy himself that all are properly accounted for.*
>
> *In the event that the client himself handles the payment of bond interest coupons and actual payment of the bonds, it will be necessary for the auditor to examine all bonds which have been paid and cancelled during the audit period, and also examine and account for all interest coupons which have been paid or which should have been paid during the audit period.*

The notes payable general ledger controlling account should be carefully analyzed to determine that there is no pattern of "window dressing." This is frequently accomplished by paying off notes just prior to the audit date and reborrowing the money at a subsequent date. Any indication of such a pattern should be carefully investigated to determine that such transactions are legitimate and in the normal course of business.

REQUIREMENTS OF SPECIAL SITUATIONS

In the case of small family corporations particularly, it will be found that frequently the major stockholder will advance cash from time to time in order to permit the corporation to meet its obligations. Unless the formalities of such an advance are carefully observed, the Internal Revenue Service may consider these advances to be contributions to capital rather than loans. To avoid this situation, with the consequent loss of the interest deduction to the corporation, the auditor should satisfy himself that the following minimum steps have been taken:

1. Authorization for the loan has been fully detailed in the appropriate minutes of board of directors' meetings, and if necessary, in stockholders' meetings.
2. Notes in proper form have been made out and signed.
3. The rate of interest and the time of repayment must be clearly indicated.
4. The rate of interest and other terms must be reasonable, taking into consideration all of the elements surrounding the transaction.
5. Interest must be paid as agreed.

   Note: *The Internal Revenue Code provides that all interest accrued at the end of the taxpayer's year due to a related taxpayer, must be paid within 75 days after the close of the year or the deduction will be lost [Sec. 267 (a) (2)].*

6. In addition to the above, there may be additional conditions imposed by the state in which the corporation is situated. The corporation's attorney should be consulted in this regard.

If any of the foregoing are omitted, the auditor should advise the client accordingly. Any interest accrued and not paid within the allowable time will be disallowed on examination, with a resulting increase in income tax liability.

If, in the opinion of the auditor, "window dressing" has been resorted to, and the amount is material, the liability should be restored to the books and subsequently shown on the financial statements. If the client does not agree to such action, the auditor may find it necessary to modify his opinion, or, in extreme cases, decline to express an opinion.

FINANCIAL STATEMENT PRESENTATION

For purposes of Balance Sheet presentation, Notes Payable may be listed by their various categories, if they are material, and, depending upon the maturity of the instruments, as either current or noncurrent. It is common practice, although not universally followed, to list the current portion of Notes Payable as the first item under "Liabilities."

There is no uniform agreement among auditors as to presentation of the portions to be considered as current and noncurrent, where loans are repaid by means of a uniform monthly payment which includes interest and principal. For example, a loan is to be repaid at the rate of $1,000 per month, this payment to include interest and principal. Assume an initial loan of $100,000, with simple interest at the rate of 6 per cent per annum. The first month's payment would represent $500 interest and $500 payment on principal. The second month's payment would represent $497.50 payment on interest and $502.50 on principal, etc. The question now arises as to the correct amount to be shown as a current liability; that is, the amount due during the ensuing 12 months. Ordinarily, since future expenses to be paid from future earnings are not reflected on a balance sheet (unless they constitute actual liabilities), only the amount due on principal might be considered the correct amount to show as a current liability at the balance sheet date.

However, the more common practice appears to be to show 12 times the monthly payment as the amount due currently. Since the method of presentation has no effect on the total liability, it is more conservative to use this latter method of computing the current portion.

If assets have been pledged to secure the payment of notes, disclosure must be made upon the balance sheet by notation under the caption affected or by reference to "Notes to Financial Statements," if separate Notes are used.

Usual balance sheet presentation is as follows:

(Under "Current Liabilities")

Notes and contracts payable:

Notes payable—Secured—Note A	$500,000
Notes payable—Unsecured	200,000
Installment contracts	10,000
Mortgage payments due within one year	100,000

Total notes and contracts payable	$810,000

If there are long-term liabilities, they may be shown as follows:

(Under "Long-Term Liabilities")

Mortgage payable—Note B	$1,000,000
Less: Current portion, above	100,000

Total long-term liabilities	$900,000

Security pledged against notes and contracts payable can be explained in "Notes to Financial Statements" similar to the following:

Note A: The Corporation has pledged all of its accounts receivable to the Blank National Bank, as security for a loan evidenced by promissory notes, the balance due thereon being $500,000 at the balance sheet date. The original amount of the loan was $600,000, bears interest at the rate of 7 per cent per annum, and is due on December 15, 19xx.

Note B: On April 21, 19xx the Corporation borrowed $1,500,000 from the LMN Life Insurance Company, and has issued its note therefor due in annual installments of $100,000 plus interest at the rate of 6 per cent per annum on the unpaid balance; all land and buildings owned by the Corporation have been pledged thereagainst.

Notes and contracts payable are of utmost interest to all credit grantors. It is highly desirable to prepare a detailed schedule of all notes, mortgages, and contracts, showing all of the pertinent information, for inclusion in the Supplemental Information section of the audit report. This will enable the bank or other credit grantor to secure this most important information concerning the ability of the client to meet his obligations as they mature. This information is essential to any granting of credit and will have to be supplied either by the auditor or his client in order to secure credit. The following schedule is one form often used:

DETAIL OF NOTES PAYABLE

Type of Obligation	Security	Rate of Int.	Amount Current	Amount Noncurrent
Mortgage	Land and buildings	6½%	$12,000	$188,000 [1]
Note—C/M	Truck	8%	960	1,920 [2]
Note	None	8%	. . . . . .	15,000 [3]
Note	Accounts receivable	8%	15,500	. . . . . . [4]
			$28,460	$204,920

[1] INM Life Insurance Company—payable $3,000 quarterly, together with interest on unpaid balance.

[2] Blank National Bank—payable $80 per month, including interest.

[3] Stockholders, due February 15, 19zz—interest payable semiannually; principal payment subordinated to payment of all amounts owing to Blank National Bank.

[4] Blank National Bank—payments received on pledged accounts receivable deposited in special restricted bank account as received; balance of principal, if any, due October 28, 19xx.

Figure 9-3

Monthly schedule of principal payments:

October	$15,580
November	80
December	3,080
January	80

February	80
March	3,080
April	80
May	80
June	3,080
July	80
August	80
September	3,080
	$28,460

10

Auditing Trade
Accounts Payable

For small and medium-sized companies, trade accounts usually constitute the most numerous and often the largest total current liability. Confirmation of trade accounts payable is by direct correspondence with the creditor by means of either a "positive" or "negative" confirmation request. One important element in confirming accounts payable is to mail the requests sufficiently early so that adequate follow-up can be made on those requests which are not answered, and which are considered to be material.

Trade accounts payable, as the term is generally understood, will include all billing made by creditors for goods and services. This will include not only bills for merchandise, but also for services such as legal, accounting, and other professional services, utilities, rents, insurance, and similar items. Ordinarily, only those items which have actually been invoiced will be included in this category. Accruals, not invoiced, are treated in Chapter 11, "Auditing Accrued Taxes and Other Expenses."

The size, quantity, and type of accounts payable will vary greatly, of course, from one business enterprise to another. Organizations dealing primarily with services such as insurance and employment agencies, professional groups such as physicians, attorneys, and architects, will usually have as accounts payable only invoices for office supplies and expenses, rent, and in the case of insurance agencies, premiums due for policies delivered to clients. On the other hand, mercantile and manufacturing firms can be expected to have substantial accounts payable for merchandise and material as well as operating supplies.

While all auditing procedures are determined to a considerable degree by information developed by the examination of the system of internal control, discussed in Chapter 3, "Examining the System of Internal Control," trade accounts payable, particularly in small and medium-sized businesses, present some special problems which are discussed below.

Small and medium-sized concerns usually follow one of two procedures in accounting for accounts payable. The more common is a detail ledger with an account for each creditor, to which is posted the invoices received and the payments made, with a controlling account in the general ledger. The second method is to use a voucher register in which is listed all of the invoices as they are received. Two extra columns are provided, one for check number and one for date of the check. As payments are made, the check number and date are entered in the voucher register to show that payment has been made. Accordingly, therefore, the open items represent unpaid accounts, and at the end of each month, the open items are listed and totalled, usually on an adding machine. The total should agree with the controlling account in the general ledger. A variation of the second method, often encountered when key-driven accounting machines are used, is to enter the unpaid invoices as received on the voucher portion of a voucher check, and when payment is made, the check is completed and pulled from the pending file.

The problem for the auditor is to satisfy himself that whatever system is used, all accounts payable are properly entered. Unfortunately, most small businesses do not have a separate receiving department, so that receiving records are seldom available for verification and tracing to vendors' invoices. Under such circumstances, it is easy for an invoice to be omitted inadvertently or even deliberately. In the case of a subsequent audit, comparison with prior years' figures is the first procedure. Omission of a creditor usually appearing in previous years' accounts can be the subject of further investigation. It is considered good auditing practice to send requests for confirmation of accounts payable to creditors usually having open accounts, even if the books show no liability at the audit date.

On the first audit, the auditor will have to depend upon careful scrutiny of all of the pertinent data; purchase orders (which, again unfortunately, are not often conscientiously used by small businesses); receiving reports, if any; correspondence with vendors or prospective vendors; and similar information.

AUDIT PROGRAM

Prior to the Audit Date

1. Scrutinize the accounts payable ledger or such other records as the client may maintain, to determine the approximate quantity of confirmations which will be sent.

2. Prepare requests for confirmation and note on trial balance creditors to whom requests were mailed.

3. Mail requests for confirmation, which may include a request for statement of account, preferably a few days prior to the audit date. This permits the vendor to mail the usual monthly statement direct to the auditor rather than to the client.

As of Audit Date

1. Make a careful cutoff of receiving reports so that it will be possible to determine that all merchandise which has been received by the audit date is reflected in accounts payable. This is treated in greater detail in Chapter 6, "Auditing Inventories."

Subsequent to Audit Date

1. Prepare a trial balance of accounts payable, aged by month, in which the purchase was made. (The trial balance may be prepared shortly before the audit date so that a record of confirmation requests can be noted directly upon it. Even when the trial balance is made subsequent to the audit date some adjustments are almost inevitable, so that preparing it early seldom results in additional audit time.)

2. Verify that requests for confirmation have been mailed to all accounts which it has been determined should be confirmed.

3. Compare information shown by returned confirmation requests with amounts shown by the client and reconcile any differences.

4. Follow up on any requests for confirmation which have not been returned and which are considered to be material.

5. Make any necessary adjusting entries and post to general ledger.

WORKING PAPERS REQUIRED

Trade Accounts Payable

Prepare trial balance, showing name of creditor, amount due, and the month in which the billing was made. For example, assuming a September 30th audit date, the first money column would show the total amount due, then the next column would show the amount billed in September; the next column the amount billed in August, the next column July, etc. Figure 10-1 shows a satisfactory example of a trial balance (page 136, 137).

If there should be any security for the account payable, a situation rather rarely encountered, it would be noted on the trial balance. In reviewing the trade accounts payable, the auditor should be on the alert to determine whether or not there is any merchandise consigned, and if such consigned merchandise does appear on the inventory it should be traced back to the proper documents. Consigned inventories are treated in detail in Chapter 6, "Auditing Inventories."

All correspondence together with any "positive" confirmation requests returned by creditors, should be filed with the working papers. In those instances where the volume is large and the size of the forms is not convenient for filing with the audit working papers, a separate file may be set up, with a suitable notation in the working papers giving the location of the special file.

XYZ CORPORATION
ACCOUNTS PAYABLE
9 - 30 - 19XX

		TOTAL	BILLED IN SEPTEMBER	AUGUST	JULY	PRIOR
ABLE, BAKER & CARR		25000		25000		
ADAMS + COMPANY		125000	100000	12500	12500	
BROWN CORP.		97500	97500			
BURLEIGH + CO.		124700	124700			
CATT & FIDDLE		43000	43000			
DAVIS AND SONS		79000	50000			29000
		2800000	2000000	500000	200000	100000

Figure 10-1

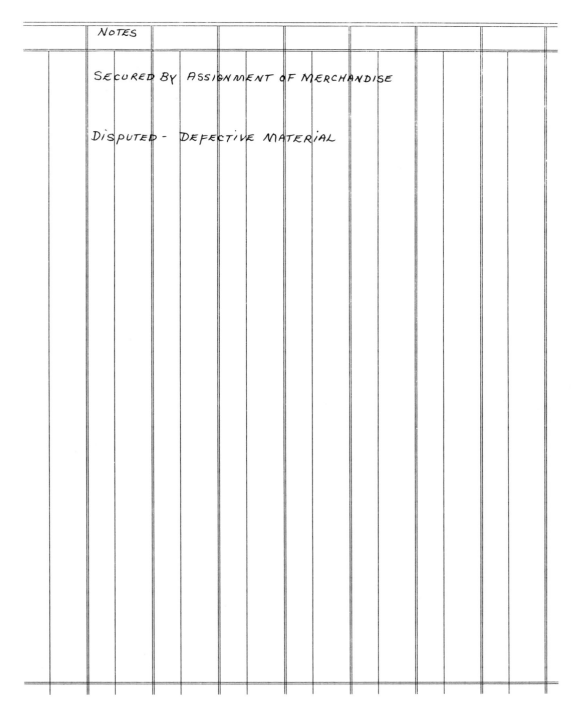

Figure 10-1 (contd.)

METHOD OF VERIFICATION

Trade Accounts Payable

The only satisfactory method of confirming accounts payable is by direct correspondence with the creditor. Requests for confirmation, as is the case with accounts receivable, may be either by the "positive" method—in which case the creditor is asked to reply directly to the auditor, stating whether or not the amount shown by the debtor is correct, or by the "negative" method—in which case a statement is sent to the creditor stating that the books of the debtor show a certain amount as being owed at the balance sheet date, and that if the auditor does not hear from the creditor it will be assumed to be correct. It is more satisfactory to use a positive request for confirmation.

It is not possible to set a specific percentage of accounts payable which should be confirmed. Obviously, where there is good internal control, and no discrepancies have been noted, the auditor is justified in confirming fewer accounts than if the reverse were true. As a guideline, however, the following may have merit: assume total accounts payable of $25,000; approximately 150 different accounts, with 20 creditors accounting for $15,000 of the total. Obviously, the 20 major accounts would be confirmed by "positive" confirmations. Of the remaining 130 accounts, all of those showing balances under, say, $100 would be omitted and "negative" requests for confirmation sent to the remainder. If no significant differences were reported, then the confirmation may be considered satisfactory. If, however, an appreciable number of differences were reported, it would be advisable to make a complete confirmation of the accounts payable.

If the confirmations are sent shortly before the audit date, it is not always possible to put in the amount, since all invoices may not yet have been received by the client. In this case, the amount space is simply left blank and the creditor is asked to fill it in. Inasmuch as the creditor has a very distinct interest in letting the auditor know the amount due, he will usually respond quite promptly. Therefore, confirmation requests with the amounts blank are usually quite satisfactory. Some auditors use a printed form, others use a form letter. If a form letter is used, it is preferably put on the client's stationery and should be signed by an officer of the client company. Following is a satisfactory form of such a letter:

Gentlemen:

   In connection with our regular audit, will you please confirm directly to our auditors, Able, Baker, and Carr, 1000 Central Avenue, Our Town, State, the amount due you as of September 30, 19xx.

Amount due you $_____

Very truly yours,

XYZ Company

By _____
Treasurer

The above amount is correct.

Signed _____ Date

The above is *not* correct. Difference is as follows:

Signed _____ Date

If the auditor uses his own printed form, the name of the client is rubber-stamped or typed in and, of course, the date for which confirmation is requested (audit date). Again it is suggested that no request for confirmation be sent out, except when signed by a responsible officer of the client company, in order to encourage a prompt and satisfactory response. In all events, a stamped and addressed envelope must accompany the request for confirmation.

If the client is an enterprise which customarily has consigned merchandise, or has secured accounts payable, or in some other manner varies from the norm, the confirmation request in letter form should be enlarged to include the additional information. For example, the following could be used:

Gentlemen:

In connection with our regular audit, will you please confirm directly to our auditors, Able, Baker, and Carr, 1000 Central Avenue, Our Town, State, the following information in regard to our account with you as of September 30, 19xx:

Total amount due	$_____
Total amount on consignment (*not* included in the above)	$_____
Security (if any)	_____
Date above amount(s) are or will be due	_____

Very truly yours,

XYZ Company

By _____
                                    Treasurer

Some auditors use a combination form for confirming both accounts receivable and accounts payable. The wording of the request section is usually similar to the following:

Amount we owe you $_____

Amount you owe us $_____

Since in only rare instances is one company both debtor and creditor, the only justification for using a combination form is that its use eliminates one printed form. In the opinion of the author, however, this minor saving is more than offset by the confusion caused by the use of a combination form, often resulting in additional correspondence being required to secure adequate confirmation.

The client may be requested to retain all monthly statements of account which are received for the period ending with the audit date. Since employees of the client have ample opportunity either to alter or to destroy incoming statements of account, they cannot be relied upon without additional confirmation. However, they do constitute useful data, particularly for those accounts which are considered too small to justify a "positive" confirmation.

REQUIREMENTS OF SPECIAL SITUATIONS

The auditor should be aware that there is always the possibility that evidence of accounts payable may be deliberately kept from his notice. It would be impracticable, if not impossible, to take all of the steps necessary to completely eliminate the possibility of a conspiracy between two or more employees of a small business to conceal accounts payable. There are, however, some procedures which can be followed in addition to those discussed under "Method of Verification" earlier in this chapter. One method is to make a careful comparison of percentage of cost of sales between the year being audited and the prior year. Any difference should be explained. Another is the comparison between expenses for two or more years. For example, a material decrease in rent expense may mean that one month's rent was omitted. Another procedure that may be justified in some circumstances, is to trace payments made to creditors during the first one or two months following the close of the prior fiscal year, to see exactly what invoices were being paid. If the invoices being paid were for material or services delivered during the prior fiscal year, the invoices should have been included in accounts payable as of the close of that year. If they were not included, the auditor would have reason to be suspicious of the accounts payable as of the end of the current year.

FINANCIAL STATEMENT PRESENTATION

Unless deferred beyond one year by special arrangement, trade accounts payable constitute a current liability and are usually shown following "Notes Payable" on the balance sheet. This is by no means a universally accepted convention, and "Accounts Payable—Trade" is frequently shown as the first item under "Current Liabilities." The exact position is probably not too important and will vary with the personal preference of the auditor as well as conforming with previous financial statement presentation. Conforming with earlier statements is always desirable unless the earlier statements are demonstrably incorrect.

In the supplemental information section, it is highly desirable to furnish an aging of accounts payable of the client in this respect. It is also quite useful to show amounts for the previous year together with the percentages. This gives a good indication of the trend of payments, a most useful indicator. Following is one suggested form of presenting this information in the supplemental information section; if one creditor, or a very small group of creditors represent a material amount of the total, this fact should be noted.

ACCOUNTS PAYABLE—TRADE

	September 30,			
	19xx		*19xy*	
	Amount	%	Amount	%
Billed during:				
September	$20,000 [1]	71.4	$24,000 [1]	70.6
August	5,000	17.9	6,000	17.6
July	2,000	7.1	3,000	8.8
Prior	1,000 [2]	3.6	1,000	3.0
Total	$28,000	100.0	$34,000	100.0

Note: [1] Of this total, $10,000 was due to the W Company as of September 30, 19xx, and $9,000 as of September 30, 19xy.

[2] This amount is in dispute pending the settlement of certain freight claims, but represents the greatest liability that can accrue to the company.

11

Auditing Accrued Taxes
and Other Expenses

Every business enterprise has accrued taxes and expenses as of the audit date. For convenience, accrued taxes may be broken down into the following general categories:

1. Payroll taxes.
2. Withheld taxes and other employee deductions.
3. Income taxes.
4. Sales taxes.
5. Property taxes.
6. Excise taxes.
7. Miscellaneous licenses and fees.

Virtually all businesses at the present time are subject to federal FICA taxes and federal and state unemployment compensation taxes. In some states, workman's compensation insurance is administered by a state agency, rather than a private insurance carrier, and it is customary in these states to include accrued premiums as a part of accrued payroll taxes. From a theoretical standpoint, there is no difference between premiums payable to a governmental agency and premiums payable to a private insurance carrier, but custom in those jurisdictions having a state-operated agency usually dictates that the accrued premiums be included with accrued payroll taxes for financial statement presentation. The distinction is usually unimportant.

Withholding taxes are required by every employer for federal income taxes. In many states the employer is also required to withhold a state income tax, and in some cases statutory withholdings for hospitalization, health, and welfare payments as well.

In addition to statutory withholdings, some organizations have withholdings for union dues and assessments; for profit sharing contributions; for credit union payments or savings; and in some instances, liens which may have been filed against an employee in the form of a wage garnishment.

Some public accountants draw a distinction between withheld taxes (representing the employee's portion) and accrued payroll taxes (representing the employer's portion) and show them separately on the balance sheet. Theoretically such a distinction exists, but in practice it is completely immaterial, and unless there is some special reason for so doing, it merely clutters the financial statements. Present Internal Revenue Code provisions permit the corporate veil to be pierced and a personal liability attached to any corporate officer responsible for the payment of federal income taxes withheld or for FICA taxes withheld and due from the employer and not paid to the Treasury Department—these provisions make no distinctions between funds withheld from employees and funds due from the employer. Other employee deductions also may take the form of constructive trust funds, and in some jurisdictions may impose a personal liability upon the responsible corporate officer for negligence if the funds are not promptly paid over.

Corporations having a taxable income for the period will show a liability for federal income tax, and in the event of such a tax, a state income tax as well. In this connection, it should be noted that subchapter S corporations are not subject to the federal income tax, but may have a liability for state or local income taxes.

Sales taxes are imposed by most states and many smaller governmental agencies. While the auditor is expected to be knowledgeable about taxes, some of the problems involved in determining sales tax liability, particularly in interstate commerce, become highly legal in nature, and the auditor or his client should have proper legal advice as to the applicability of the law to the particular situation. Having determined the liability of the client for the tax, the auditor is then in a position to verify that the amount of the liability accrued at the balance sheet date is correct.

Property taxes will be accrued in nearly every instance, since almost without exception, taxes for real and personal property are levied in every jurisdiction.

Over the years, excise taxes have been largely in the province of the federal government and have ranged over the complete area of business activity. The recent trend, however, has been for Congress to eliminate excise taxes from most transactions commonly entered into by small and medium-sized businesses. Accordingly, while a number of excise taxes are in effect, and undoubtedly the situation will change with each Congress, most smaller businesses are not burdened with excise taxes. Unfortunately, in many states, as the federal government eliminated excise taxes, the states and other governmental agencies have imposed such taxes. The auditor will necessarily be familiar with the excise tax laws of his particular state.

Lastly, there are licenses and other statutory fees, which may be accrued if material. In many instances, however, such fees and licenses are relatively small and, therefore, immaterial on the financial statements, and accordingly are often expensed when paid.

It is somewhat more difficult to categorize expenses which may have accrued at the balance sheet date. These will vary widely with different types of business concerns, but usually will represent services rather than merchandise, the reason being that customarily, when merchandise is shipped it is billed as of the date of shipment, and, therefore, will appear as an account payable rather than an accrued expense.

An exception to this general rule will be found whenever consigned merchandise is held by a client. As of the audit date it may be determined that portions of the consigned inventory have been sold, and a liability to the vendor thereby exists, but that the actual invoicing has not yet been prepared and will not appear in accounts payable. However, in such cases it is common practice to proceed on the theory that the invoice has been made and to include the liability in accounts payable, rather than accrued liabilities.

The following summary is not to be considered all-inclusive but is a general outline of the accrued expenses which the auditor should be alert to determine:

1. Rent.
2. Utilities.
3. Professional services, such as legal and accounting.
4. Insurance.
5. Commissions.
6. Salaries and wages.
7. Interest.
8. Reserves.

For convenience, reserves may be broken down into the following four categories:

1. Asset revaluation

Such revaluation accounts are commonly carried as a reduction of the asset on the balance sheet. Examples are "Allowance for Depreciation" and "Allowance for Bad Debts."

2. Surplus reserves

These are reserves set up by appropriate action, usually by the board of directors or stockholders, against one or more elements of stockholders' equity. Such a reserve might be a reserve for conversion into common stock, for example, by holders of preferred stock or debentures or other debt instruments. Current auditing procedures require that a notation on the balance sheet be made, either by a footnote or by an actual figure under the appropriate caption, so that a reader of the balance sheet is aware of the possible dilution of the common stock. This is particularly appropriate when it is remembered that per share earnings are based on actual outstanding shares at the balance sheet date, but that the earnings per share may be changed very materially should holders of other securities convert their holdings into common stock. While such is not often encountered in small and medium-sized businesses it is a situation for which the auditor must be alert.

Another reserve often found in the stockholders' equity section of the balance sheet is the "appropriated" reserve. This constitutes a reserve in the truest sense, since it is "reserved" by action of the board of directors for a specific purpose, often for the purpose of acquiring new or additional fixed assets. The value of the use of reserve accounts within the stockholders' equity accounts is to give notice to readers that retained earnings, normally available for the payment of dividends, have been restricted, and thus cannot be used for the payment of dividends.

3. Reserves against debt

The most common form of this type of reserve is the sinking fund. Loans, notably those evidenced by bonds or debentures, may require that certain funds be set aside periodically for the purpose of making payment upon the debt. Often the amount of the reserve is determined by the profit earned, and frequently the form in which the reserve is to be held is specified. For example, funds representing the reserve may be required to be held in a special restricted bank account, or funds may be used to acquire bonds or other debt instruments pending their actual delivery to the trustee for cancellation. When such funds are held under specified restrictions, and cannot be used for any other purpose, it is customary to show them as a reduction of the applicable liability, an exception to the general rule that assets should not be applied to reduce specific liabilities.

4. Reserves used to indicate liability

There is often only a tenuous difference between a reserve of this nature and an accrual. Reserves may be said to differ from accruals principally in that a reserve, while representing an actual liability, represents a liability that cannot be definitely determined in amount until some future date. The liability exists at the audit date, and therefore must be disclosed in the financial statements, even if the amount is an estimation. An example of a proper reserve of this nature would be a reserve for guarantees and warranties. At the balance sheet date it is known that sums will have to be spent to make good guarantees and warranties for merchandise sold during the fiscal period just ended, but the exact amount cannot be determined until some future date. Nevertheless, assuming that the amount is expected to be significant, it would be improper to omit from the financial statements the liability and the expense. A reserve account solves this problem.

In this regard, a purely contingent liability can be further distinguished in that the contingent liability represents a possible liability that may occur, but which, at the audit date is not expected to occur. For example, the client may be the defendant in a lawsuit, but any probable damages as well as legal and court costs are adequately covered by insurance. Thus, at the audit date it does not appear likely that the client will have any out-of-pocket expenses in connection with the suit. Nevertheless, there is always the remote possibility that some unforeseen circumstance may cause the client to have to pay damages and costs. Accordingly, the auditor must make full disclosure of the circumstances, but since the liability appears to be purely a contingent one, no reserve would be set up.

If, at the audit date, the management knows that funds will be required to make payments for vacations, insurance benefits, and other items, which have accrued at the audit date but where amounts cannot be exactly determined, a reserve may be employed rather than setting up an accrual. Another example of a reserve is the situation where a wage dispute exists, and the company has an undetermined liability for wages due under a labor contract in process of negotiation, but with retroactive provisions. Under such circumstances a reserve would be required.

Under normal circumstances, however, for small and medium-sized organizations, there is usually adequate information available so that the amount of the liability can be determined reasonably accurately and can, therefore, be included as an accrued expense rather than a reserve. It is nearly always preferable to make an accrual rather than to set up a reserve.

Treatment of reserves for federal income tax purposes varies with the nature of the reserve. For example, assuming that the client is on a reserve basis for bad debts, all charges to the reserve for bad debts for the fiscal period are allowed as a deduction under Internal Revenue Service regulations. Other reserves, however, such as for vacations, warranty expense, and similar items have been the subject of considerable controversy, the position of the Internal Revenue Service usually being that no deduction is allowable until the expense has actually been paid. This is another instance of conservative auditing procedure and income tax treatment being at variance.

Basic auditing procedures for accrued taxes and expenses consist of a careful review, test, and check of the appropriate data. In some cases it is possible to confirm amounts directly, but ordinarily direct confirmation is not practicable with accrued taxes and expenses.

In addition to actual accrued expenses and reserves, there are often contingent liabilities for services to be rendered in future periods.

Contingent liabilities for leases, service contracts, etc.

Leases for equipment, which may be considered as purchases are treated in detail in Chapter 8, "Auditing Fixed Assets." However, in addition to leases of this nature, many businesses have lease agreements for the use of factory premises, office space, and short-term leases for equipment, including computer hardware. Any rentals due as of the audit date will have been accrued under the appropriate account and treated as accrued liabilities. The client obviously has a contingent liability for future periods of time for such leases. Notation should be made and all leases carefully scrutinized to determine whether or not the amount is significant. Contingent liabilities are not ordinarily included as actual liabilities and reflected on the books, but if material in amount they must be covered by a note to the financial statement.

In the same manner, service contracts should also be examined. Many of these service contracts are nominal in amount and usually can be cancelled with little or no penalty on relatively short notices. Such contracts would cover servicing of office machines and equipment, janitorial service, and similar items. These are usually of too small an amount to be considered significant, and since they constitute an ordinary business expense are generally omitted from notation. However, more recently extensive service contracts, particularly for the use of computer services, have come into being.

These should be carefully scrutinized and if the amount warrants, should be included with leases and any other contingent liabilities of this nature.

AUDIT PROGRAM

Subsequent to Audit Date

1. Review all payroll tax and withholding returns, federal, state, and local (if any).
2. Trace total payroll as shown by the payroll tax returns to the payroll summary and verify that the amounts agree with the amounts shown by the payroll records.
3. Verify the actual payment, subsequent to the audit date, of all accrued taxes.
4. Schedule and verify computation of all recorded accrued expenses.
5. Schedule and verify all reserve accounts.
6. Schedule all leases and contracts to determine if the amounts of the contingent liability are significant.
7. Prepare and post to the working trial balance any necessary adjustments.

WORKING PAPERS REQUIRED

Accrued Payroll Taxes and Withheld Taxes

A work sheet should be prepared, showing for each payroll tax in effect, and for each payroll withholding tax, the accrual at the beginning of the year, the taxes actually paid during each calendar quarter, the accrual at the end of the year, and the expense for the year. This can be done using a separate work sheet for each tax or by using a summary sheet. A summary work sheet has the advantage, in that the entire payroll tax expense can be shown on one schedule. Figure 11-1 is an example of such a work sheet.

In addition to showing the payroll taxes paid, the summary should also show the amount of the taxable payroll. If desired, the same summary sheet can be used to show the beginning and ending accruals and payments for all other employee payroll withholdings, and if any represent an additional expense for the corporation, the expense may also be included in the schedule.

> Note: *Withholdings to repay ordinary payroll advances should not be included in this category. Advances of this nature are properly handled as "Other Accounts Receivable" and are treated in detail in Chapter 5, "Auditing Receivables."*

Accrued Income Taxes Payable

In a manual of this size, space does not permit a detailed discussion of the preparation of federal income tax returns, or state and local income tax returns. The completion of a satisfactory audit will provide all of the basic and detail information necessary to prepare the income tax returns properly. If the income tax requirements

XYZ Corporation
9-30-19XX

Payroll Tax Summary

	Accrued 10-1-XX	Paid 4th Q	Paid 1st Q	Paid 2nd Q	Paid 3rd Q	Accrued 9-30-XX	Expense Year	Taxable Payroll
FICA	20000	140000	150000	160000	120000	40000	290000	6590000
Federal I.T. W/H	40000	120000	120000	120000	120000	40000	-0-	-
Federal Unemployment	14500	-	18000	-	-	14500	18000	4500000
State Unemployment	16500	30000	30000	30000	30000	17500	121000	5500000
State Income Tax W/H	8000	8000	10000	10000	10000	10000	-0-	-
Total Expense							429000	

Figure 11-1

are kept in mind as the audit progresses, much time can be saved by preparing the audit information in a form that can be used for the preparation of the income tax returns without further effort.

The original of the income tax returns and accompanying schedules are usually filed separately from the audit working papers. There are several reasons for this. First, they are voluminous and add considerably to the bulk of the file; they are often referred to independently of the audit working papers, and they are often kept in the current file longer than the regular audit working papers. However, this is a matter of personal preference and established office procedure.

The working trial balance can be adapted to permit additional columns to be used to accumulate and segregate items to be used for income tax preparation. This is described in detail in Chapter 2, "Preparation of the Working Papers." From the working trial balance, working papers can be prepared for the specific income tax return schedules. While these schedules will vary greatly from one return to another, the following are representative of those schedules required on most returns:

- Receipts and revenues, segregated by categories.
- Cost of goods sold.
- Gains and losses.
- Compensation of officers.
- Bad debts.
- Taxes.
- Contributions.
- Casualty losses.
- Depreciation.
- Depletion.
- Employees' benefit plans including pension, profit-sharing, insurance, etc.
- Operating loss deduction.
- Special deductions:

  Note: *1. "Special deductions" as listed in federal income tax returns are not often encountered in auditing small and medium-sized corporations, except for the dividends received.*

  2. Accrued items due to related taxpayers must be paid within a specified period after the close of the tax year, in order to qualify as tax deductions. The auditor must verify that such accruals have been paid on time for the prior year, and should be sure that his client is aware of this requirement for any accruals appearing on the current balance sheet.

Other Accrued Taxes

A work sheet should be prepared for each accrued tax account. If only one or two payments are made each year for a particular tax, several different accruals can be made on one work sheet. Each work sheet should show the accrual at the beginning of the year, charges and credits during the year, and the balance at the end of the year.

Accrued Expenses

A work sheet will be required for each accrued expense account, showing the balance in the account at the beginning of the year, the charges and credits to the account during the year, and the balance at the end of the year. As is true of accrued taxes, if there are only two or three entries during the year, two or more accounts may be combined on one work sheet if desired. Time can often be saved by combining like items. For example, if the debits to the accrual account during the year consist of 12 monthly cash payments, they can be combined into one single total for entry on the work sheet. If time of payment is critical, dates of payment should be traced to the cashbook or other source and notation made of any delinquent payment.

Contingent Liabilities

A work sheet should be prepared, showing for each service contract and lease the name of the lessor, nature of the lease, period of the lease, and the monthly or annual rental, together with the length of time yet to run. The total contingent liabilities should be computed. If material in amount, a separate schedule should be prepared showing the total amount of lease and other service contingency which will be included in notes to financial statements.

METHOD OF VERIFICATION

Accrued Payroll Taxes

The copy of each payroll tax return filed for the year should be reviewed and the computations verified. The total taxable payroll reported should be reconciled with the payroll amounts appearing on the payroll summary work sheet. In this connection, it is important to determine that payroll taxes due on payrolls accrued, but not paid at the audit date, are included. Ultimate payment of all payroll taxes which have been accrued at the audit date should be verified during the course of the audit. Most payroll taxes are due and will ordinarily be paid during the course of the field work, except for the Federal Unemployment Tax for those corporations not on a calendar-year basis. Cancelled checks representing payment of payroll taxes accrued at the audit date should be inspected to determine that they have actually been paid by the bank. All correspondence from taxing authorities should be carefully scrutinized for evidence of any delinquencies. In this connection, it should be noted that most tax penalties are not deductible for federal income tax purposes. Accordingly, if any penalties have been paid, disposition of the penalties should be traced to the ultimate expense account and, if necessary, adjustments should be made.

In auditing payments of payroll taxes, time of payment must be carefully noted. Tax regulations are specific as to time for payment, and the auditor should determine that payments have been made as required.

Accrued Withheld Taxes and Other Withholdings

For all practical purposes federal income taxes withheld from employees' pay are treated the same as FICA taxes, and verification can be made at the same time and in the same manner as for the payroll taxes. State and local taxes required to be withheld will be governed by the applicable laws and regulations with which the auditor is presumed to be familiar. Verification procedures would be similar to those used for federal taxes.

Withholdings, other than statutory, are governed by contract. By reference to the applicable instrument, which may be a labor contract, pension or profit-sharing agreement, credit union agreement, or similar document, the auditor should determine that any withholdings are in strict accord with the controlling instrument. In addition, some jurisdictions require that each employee personally sign an authorization before any moneys may be withheld from his pay. In this case, it will be necessary to determine that such an authorization is in the client's payroll file.

Accrued Income Taxes

The amount of the accrued federal income tax will ordinarily be the amount of the tax due for the year just ended, less amounts paid in advance. If an examination has been made of the prior year's income tax returns, the auditor should carefully review the examining agent's report. In the case of most smaller clients, the auditor is usually notified when the client is aware that an examination is to be made, and frequently the auditor is in close contact with the progress and results of the examination, if, in fact, he does not actively participate in it. Accordingly, as at the audit date, he should be aware of the status of any unexamined and still open years. If an additional assessment has resulted from such an examination, and has not been paid by the audit date, it would be included with the current year's income tax liability.

Often, particularly in the case of small and medium-sized concerns, the auditor will prepare the tax return, in which case he has effectively audited the return. If the client's staff has prepared the income tax return, the auditor will review the return and make any necessary adjustments. In most instances advance payments will have been required, and the auditor should verify that these advance payments have been made on time.

If state and/or local income tax returns are required, they would be verified in the same manner.

Accrued Sales Taxes

Sales taxes are verified by reference to copies of the returns, the taxable amounts compared with the sales or cash receipts journals, and the computations verified. The auditor is presumed to be familiar with the requirements for preparing proper sales tax returns, since they are state or local in nature. Payments of all required sales taxes should be traced to the cash disbursements journal for the year under review to insure that there are no delinquencies. If sales tax returns are required on a monthly basis, the number of months to be verified will depend to some extent upon the internal control system. If the time required to verify each month's return is material, a check of the first and last months' returns may be adequate if no differences are discovered. Often a rough check can be made by comparing the total sales for the year with the total sales tax paid for the year. This will be appropriate, of course, only when virtually all sales are subject to the tax.

Property Taxes

Most taxing agencies send tax bills showing location of the property being taxed, the assessed value, and the tax due. The auditor should make certain that the description of the property is correct, and that the tax rate applied is correct. In many cases the tax rate is shown on the tax bill, but if it is not, the auditor should secure a copy of the applicable rates and satisfy himself that the rate used is the proper one. As part of the audit of fixed assets, the auditor will usually refer to the tax bill, and the auditing of the accrued property tax can often be conveniently done at this time. It should be determined that there are no delinquencies. Usually it will be sufficient to refer to the cancelled checks representing tax payments, but if there remains any question, direct correspondence with the taxing authority is advisable.

Excise Taxes

As explained in an earlier paragraph, most federal excise taxes have been eliminated insofar as smaller businesses are concerned. However, many operations are subject to state and local excise taxes of various kinds. If any excise taxes are owed, verification of the accrual at the audit date and the expense for the year under review would be done in the same manner as that for auditing sales taxes.

Miscellaneous Licenses and Fees

An almost unlimited number of licenses, permits, and fees are imposed by state and local taxing authorities. Not only do they vary widely in nature, but their application is constantly changing. The auditor has the responsibility to keep abreast of the ones in effect in his jurisdiction at any given time. Many of them take the form of an occupation license fee, and some are similar to sales taxes, in that they are based upon gross receipts. In any event, they would be audited in the same way that sales taxes are audited. Many such licenses and fees are based upon a single annual charge. If the amount is significant, it should be accrued (or if paid in advance, set up as a prepaid expense item) and the expense reflected monthly. Any amounts so accrued as of the audit date would appear as a part of accrued taxes.

Contingent Liabilities

Contingent liability for leases and service contracts is verified by examining copies of the contracts. However, the auditor should be alert to the fact that such contracts may, in fact, exist but not be evidenced by a contract in the file. In reviewing the expense accounts, notation should be made of recurring payments which may be for leases or contract services for which no lease or contract has been found. If there is any question, direct correspondence with the payee should decide the matter.

If there are substantial leases or contracts, copies should be made for the auditor's permanent file.

REQUIREMENTS OF SPECIAL SITUATIONS

Service Organizations

Service organizations such as brokers, real estate and insurance agencies, financial institutions (other than banks), and like enterprises, are the ones most likely to have unrecorded accrued liabilities. Interest, which ordinarily is the most important element of cost likely to be omitted, can be audited in connection with notes payable, as described in Chapter 9, "Auditing Notes Payable." Payroll taxes, although often significant, are rarely overlooked, as the returns themselves constitute a reminder for the client's accountant or bookkeeper.

Professional Organizations

Occasionally, the independent accountant is called upon to audit and express an opinion on the accounts of professional partnerships and corporations, such as attorneys, doctors, architects, engineers, and others. It is customary in most businesses of this type to keep books on a cash basis, which for audit purposes must be converted to an accrual basis. Under such circumstances, the auditor must be particularly careful to see that all accrued expenses and taxes are reflected in the records. The auditing procedure used in setting up such accounts would be the same as those described earlier in this chapter.

FINANCIAL STATEMENT PRESENTATION

Almost all accrued liabilities will constitute current liabilities and will be shown in that section of the balance sheet. Accrued taxes should be segregated from accrued expenses unless one or the other is completely insignificant, in which case they may be combined under the caption "Accrued Taxes and Expenses." Accrued income taxes, however, should always be shown separately upon the balance sheet.

Reserves would be listed as either current liabilities, or as noncurrent liabilities, depending on their nature. Contingent liabilities would be covered in a footnote, or if sufficiently important, may require a paragraph in the opinion itself. This is treated in detail in Chapter 1, "Purposes of the Audit and the Auditor's Responsibility."

Supplemental Information

It is advisable to supply in the supplemental information part of the report complete detail as to any contingent liabilities which might exist. An example might be contingent liability arising out of an automobile or truck accident. Ordinarily, such liability as may exist is covered by insurance. The wording in the supplemental information report might read as follows:

> The corporation is defendant in a personal injury and property damage suit arising out of a collision on January 15, 19xx, with one of its trucks. In the opinion of counsel, any judgement likely to be rendered against the company together with all legal and court costs appears to be adequately covered by in-insurance.

Another example of disclosure in the supplemental information section might be as follows:

> The company is defendant in a suit alleging breach of contract and defective merchandise. In the opinion of counsel, the suit is without merit and it is not expected that any material cost will arise out of this action. The company carries product's and contractor's liability insurance which is expected to cover the cost of defending the suit.

Accrued Income Taxes

Complete information regarding the accrued income taxes should be given. For example:

Federal income tax accrued for year ended Sept. 30, 19xx	$50,000
Less: Prepayments	40,000
	10,000
Additional assessment for year ended Sept. 30, 19xx	1,000
Total federal income tax accrued	11,000
State income tax accrued for year ended Sept. 30, 19xx	1,000
Total accrued income tax	$12,000

Accrued Taxes—Other

Where the taxes constitute an item of any materiality it is advisable to show in the supplementary information section a breakdown of the various taxes. Following might be a suitable form:

State and federal payroll taxes	$2,500
Federal unemployment tax	240
State unemployment tax	970
Accrued federal income taxes withheld	2,400
Accrued state and local income taxes withheld	590
Accrued sales taxes	220
Real estate and personal property taxes	400
	$7,320

Notation should be made if there are any delinquencies.

Accrued Expenses

In a similar manner, it is advisable to show a breakdown of accrued expenses if the amount is significant. Following is an example of how this can be done:

Accrued insurance premiums	$ 400
Accrued interest	180
Accrued commissions	390
Accrued rent	2,000
Total	$2,970

Note: *Interest would ordinarily be shown separately on the balance sheet unless it is a minor item. Similarly, salaries and wages are always shown as a separate item unless completely immaterial.*

Contingent Liabilities

Contingent liabilities should be covered in "Notes to Financial Statements" on the balance sheet section. Following is a suggested method:

The Company is contingently liable for the remainder of a lease on the premises occupied as office and warehouse at the rate of $500 per month, payable monthly in advance. This lease running until January 1, 19yy, the total amount of such contingent liability amounting to $6,500 at the balance sheet date.

12

Auditing Capital
Accounts

In the United States, the three most common types of business organizations are: proprietorship, partnership, and corporation. While numerically proprietorships represent by far the largest portion of total businesses, it is seldom that they are audited. One reason is that most proprietorships are small, and any credit granted, either by suppliers or by banks, is usually based less upon formal financial statements than upon other factors, including assets which may be pledged as security for the credit granted. Another reason is, that in making such an audit, the auditor would be bound to determine all liabilities whether reflected on the books or not, and since this would include all of the personal obligations of the proprietor, as well as those of his wife and other members of the family for whom he may be legally liable, it is seldom practicable to conduct such an audit.

While partnerships represent some of the same hazards to the issuance of an unrestricted accountant's opinion, at least the books and records are usually kept on a more formal and complete basis. These records are required for the purpose of preparing federal income tax returns, if for no other. Also most partnerships are based upon a written instrument, and in many jurisdictions a public filing of such instrument is required, so that the auditor may have a somewhat better foundation upon which to base his audit. Additionally, while the partner has a personal liability for the debts of the partnership, his own personal debts do not have a claim against the assets of the partnership in excess of the partner's capital account therein. Thus the auditor is usually spared from having to attempt to make an audit of the personal liabilities of each partner and his family.

A variation of the partnership is the syndicate or joint venture. While there may be minor differences between the joint venture and the syndicate, essentially they are both limited partnerships. The exact legal distinctions will vary from one state to another. In most states, corporations and partnerships, as well as individuals, may be members of the joint venture, the syndicate, and the partnership. Joint ventures are common in the oil and gas exploration and development field, and syndicates are common in the real-estate holding area. Most joint ventures and syndicates are managed by an individual or organization elected by the members, and audits are very often required. The amount of capital contribution will often vary quite widely between the various members of the group, so that in auditing the capital accounts, distribution of the profit or loss to the various members' capital accounts is of prime importance.

The third common form of business enterprise is the corporation. In most states it is a relatively simple and inexpensive procedure to incorporate a small business, if stock is not to be sold to others than the incorporators. This is the type of organization the auditor is most likely to encounter among small and medium-sized businesses.

In addition to the three common forms of business enterprises, that is, sole proprietorship, partnership, and corporations, the auditor will from time to time encounter two additional businesses which he may be called upon to audit. This is the trust, which will occasionally operate a for-profit business, and the estate, which will often operate the business of a deceased person. Other than accounting for the capital accounts, there is virtually no difference in the audit procedures and the auditor's responsibility among the various types of organizations.

As outlined in Chapter 1, "Purposes of the Audit and the Auditor's Responsibility," the auditor is often called upon to conduct audits of not-for-profit organizations. Many of these, including governmental agencies, will have capital accounts in the sense that they are accountable for property. While this is not capital in the same sense as stockholder's equity, it would be audited basically in the same manner as a for-profit enterprise. While the emphasis of this chapter will be upon the auditing of for-profit organizations, under "Requirements of Special Situations" will be suggestions for auditing the comparable accounts of nonprofit organizations.

AUDIT PROGRAM

Subsequent to Audit Date

Sole proprietorship:

    1. Analyze the capital account and the drawing account.

    2. Prepare and post any necessary adjusting journal entries.

Partnership:

    1. Analyze partners' capital accounts and drawing accounts.

    2. Prepare and post any necessary adjusting journal entries.

Corporation:

1. Analyze the capital stock accounts. If there is more than one capital stock account, then an analysis must be made of each capital stock account.

2. Analyze the retained earnings account.

3. Analyze any other stockholder's equity account.

4. Prepare and post any necessary adjusting journal entries.

WORKING PAPERS REQUIRED

Capital Accounts

Working papers will be required to analyze the proprietor's or partner's capital accounts. In many instances, it will be found that there are only two or three entries per year. They will show the credit for the income earned (or charge for losses incurred) and charge for the drawings made. It is quite practicable to take the work papers from the prior year's audit and use them for the current year, adding such changes as may have occurred in the interim.

In the case of the first audit of a partnership, careful attention must be paid to the partnership agreement, to determine that all credits to the capital accounts of the partners and all withdrawals are being made in strict compliance with the partnership agreement.

The working papers should also provide for the information necessary to prepare the federal income tax return. This information changes from year to year so that it is not practicable to prepare a detail listing of the information required.

Capital Stock Accounts

A trial balance should be prepared showing for each class of capital stock (if more than one) the following information:

1. Stock certificate number.

2. Date issued.

3. Name of stockholder.

4. Number of shares.

This trial balance can easily be transferred from one year's work papers to the next, as changes occur rather seldom.

Retained Earnings

A work sheet will be required, showing the balance at the beginning of the year, additions and deductions in detail, and balance at the end of the year. Usually the

number of entries in this account are very small, so that the work sheet can be transferred from the prior year's audit file to the current year's file.

Other Surplus Accounts

A work sheet should be prepared for each general ledger account in this category. Small and medium-sized businesses do not often have accounts of this nature,
and when they do the accounts do not often change from one year to another.
Accordingly, the work papers can be transferred from one year to the next. The
following information should be shown for each such account:

1. Date of transaction.
2. Nature of transaction.
    Note: *Reference may be made to documents which may be in the permanent file, such
    as minutes of directors' meetings, stockholders' authorizations, contracts, etc.
    It is not necessary to abstract the information, reference is sufficient.*
3. Amount.

METHOD OF VERIFICATION

Capital Accounts

The capital accounts for sole proprietorships and for partnerships can be verified
by tracing the entries in the account to either the cash disbursements record or cash
receipts record for withdrawals or additional contributions to capital. The entry
representing the distribution of the income or expense for the year would, of course,
be verified from the final profit and loss statement. In this connection, it is necessary
to verify any entries representing items other than cash. For example, occasionally a
proprietor will take merchandise out of inventory for his own use. In addition to
verifying the value, it should be kept in mind that such entries are required to be reflected in the federal income tax return, on schedule C. Similar verification should be
made in the case of a partnership for any partner withdrawing merchandise or other
property of the partnership. In the case of a partnership, all withdrawals, whether of
cash or other assets of the partnership, should be evidenced by minutes of the partnership or other documentary evidence. One of the purposes of an audit of a partnership
is to insure that each partner be aware of the transactions which have occurred during
the period under review, and the withdrawals of the various partners is an integral part
of this view.

Capital Stock

Every state has certain statutory provisions for the issuance of corporation
charters. For corporations other than banking, insurance, finance, and certain other

specific categories, the issuance of a charter is usually a very simple matter. Each jurisdiction does, however, have various restrictions on the issuance of capital stock. Aside from state statutes, the Securities and Exchange Commission has certain restrictions upon the issuance of stock which is to be sold to the general public. It is assumed that the auditor will be familiar generally with the requirements of his particular state. In the case of a first audit, it would be necessary to examine the charter or such other evidence of proper incorporation; it may be advisable to confirm with the corporation's attorney that all requirements have been met, and that the corporation is legally constituted to do business.

Confirm directly with the proper state agency that the corporation has filed all required periodical reports and paid all required fees and taxes, and is in good standing as of the audit date. If there are specific requirements for the issuance of capital stock, the auditor should verify that all requirements have been complied with. Since most small and medium-sized companies issue stock rather rarely, this need be done only upon the occasion of a first audit or upon the issuance of additional stock during the period covered by the audit.

Prior to January 1, 1966, when the tax was repealed, there was a federal documentary stamp tax on the issuance and transfer of corporation capital stock for virtually all for-profit corporations. It is necessary for the auditor to verify that the tax has been paid and that the required stamps are affixed to all documents for transactions occurring prior to January 1, 1966. In addition, many states and occasionally other political subdivisions require similar stamps. It is assumed that the auditor is familiar with the requirements of his particular state.

Occasionally, a corporation will purchase its own stock. Most state laws require that any such purchases be made only out of retained earnings, so that if such a transaction has been made the auditor must verify that it has been done in conformity with state statutes. Actual certificates may or may not be issued for treasury stock, it is not material. All purchases and sales of treasury stock will require board of directors' approval, and in some cases approval of the stockholders, and will be reflected in the minute book. If a purchase is made in excess of par or stated value, the amount in excess is usually charged to retained earnings, unless there is already on the books a capital surplus arising from the sale of capital stock at a price above par or stated value, in which case the excess paid may be charged to this latter account. If treasury stock is purchased for less than par or stated value, the difference is credited to capital surplus arising from the purchase of capital stock.

Retained Earnings

Normally, entries in retained earnings accounts consist of the income or loss for the fiscal period, which is, of course, verified by auditing the income and expense accounts and the payment of dividends. Payment of dividends must be authorized by the board of directors and accordingly would be supported by minutes. Actual distribution should be verified by reference to the cash disbursements book. The auditor must satisfy himself that if a dividend has been paid, it is in accordance with any applicable statutes. For example, most states permit dividends to be paid only out of earnings. Also, if a dividend has been paid that is other than a taxable dividend to the stockholder, the auditor should determine the exact nature of the dividend, and satisfy himself that it has been properly described.

Any other entries in the retained earnings account would be verified by referring to the transactions which would be evidenced by minutes, contracts, etc.

Other Surplus Accounts

Other surplus accounts might include capital surplus, contributed surplus, revaluation surplus, and similar categories. Each would be verified by reference to the transaction upon which it is founded. These transactions would in almost every case, be authorized either by stockholders and/or board of directors, and accordingly minutes detailing the transactions would appear in the minute book. If any transactions occurred through dealings with third parties, reference would be made to any documents such as purchase agreements, financing arrangements, etc.

In this connection, it is well to watch for any options which might be granted. It is somewhat common to find that where financing has been arranged by outside parties such financing provides for the purchase of stock at some time in the future. Such option agreements will not, of course, be reflected on the books at the time, but they constitute a most important part of the financial statements and full disclosure must be made. Details of any such arrangements would normally be found in the financing agreement. The auditor should be on the alert to watch for such an option in the event that any financing has been made by the client during the period under review. Small business investment companies almost always provide for such an option, so that if there is a loan from a small business investment company the auditor would be alert to determine the nature of any option agreements.

REQUIREMENTS OF SPECIAL SITUATIONS

Capital Contributions

In reviewing the capital accounts, the auditor should keep in mind that under certain conditions the Internal Revenue Service may treat loans by stockholders as contributions to capital. This is particularly true if the loan does not carry interest or if the interest actually accrued has not been paid, and if the loan is not evidenced by proper instruments. This is treated in greater detail in Chapter 9.

Nonprofit Organizations

Nonprofit and governmental agencies do not have capital accounts in the same sense as for-profit organizations, but instead usually operate on the "Fund" system. Space does not permit an extensive discussion of fund balances but simply stated, this procedure provides that for each "Fund" (such as Endowment Fund, Operating Fund, Building Fund, etc.) there is a "Fund Balance" that, together with the liabilities, will always be equal to the total assets for that fund. This procedure provides for accountability, as well as for the use of the double-entry system of bookkeeping.

Ordinarily, there are no tangible instruments representing the balance, such as stock certificates, but rather, the ending balance is the result of transactions occurring over a period of time, in the same manner that Retained Earnings or Capital Surplus is maintained.

The use of assets from a particular fund is usually restricted to specific purposes. For example, cash in a Building Fund is normally restricted to the construction of buildings. In auditing such funds, the auditor must determine that all expenditures are in strict accordance with the purposes and authorizations applicable. In the case of hospitals, colleges, and other institutions who are the recipients of gifts, the auditor must determine that such gifts are being used in accordance with the donor's instructions. If there is any doubt, the attorney for the institution should be consulted, and his opinion followed.

FINANCIAL STATEMENT PRESENTATION

An analysis of "Retained Earnings" is usually presented as a separate schedule. It is more useful if the statement of retained earnings is made on a comparable basis for two or more years. Following is one method of such a presentation:

STATEMENT OF RETAINED EARNINGS

For the year ended September 30,

	19xx	19xw
Balance October 30,	$25,000	$20,000
Net profit for year	15,000	10,000
	40,000	30,000
Less: Dividends paid	5,000	5,000
Balance, September 30,	$35,000	$25,000

Capital stock is normally presented showing for each type of capital stock outstanding the number of shares, whether or not there is a par or stated value, etc. Treasury shares are properly shown as a deduction from the total outstanding capital stock.

Other surplus accounts are shown with appropriate captions to sufficiently describe them.

In all cases, full disclosure must be made by means of notes to the financial statements, if the information cannot conveniently be put in the caption. For example, if there is a revaluation surplus it might be designated as follows in the Notes to Financial Statements:

Note X: On January 15, 19xx, the board of directors authorized that vacant land, being held by the corporation for future expansion, which was purchased in 19yy at a cost of $2,000 an acre, be valued on the balance sheet and in the accounts of the corporation at $20,000 per acre, in accordance with an appraisal made by Mr. John Doe, certified appraiser, as of January 1, 19xx. The difference of $180,000, representing the difference between the cost and the appraisal value is treated as "Surplus Arising from Revaluation of Real Estate."

13

Auditing Income
Accounts

Income accounts are audited, first, to verify that they are in fact income, and are properly classified, and, second, to secure the information necessary to the proper preparation of the federal and other income tax returns.

The income accounts of a business will obviously vary with the type of enterprise, but for convenience can be divided into the following three general categories:

1. Regular income accounts arising through business activities normal to the business.
2. Regular but incidental income.
3. Extraordinary income.

All income arises through the sale of goods and/or services, if the term "goods" is taken in a broad sense. From an auditing standpoint, "Regular Income" would include all income which arises from the transactions normal to the business enterprise being conducted. For example, in the case of a mercantile business, ordinary income would include sales from merchandise, charges for repairs and other service, if a service department is operated, service charges for carrying accounts, if such is made, and similar transactions. In the case of a service organization, such as an insurance agency, income is primarily from commissions received from the sale of insurance policies. With professional organizations such as consulting engineers, architects, or similar firms, regular income is from the rendering of professional service. In each case, the essential point for the auditor to keep in mind is that the income is normal to the business being conducted.

Incidental income may be defined as that income which arises through normal business transactions, but which is not the primary source of income. For example, a mercantile firm may have excess funds available at certain times of the year and may invest these in short-term government or other securities and derive interest therefrom. This is normal income as opposed to extraordinary income, but is not the chief source of revenue and is merely incidental to the carrying on of regular business activities.

Extraordinary income is that which is outside of the normal business activities of the organization. For example, a company may sell land or buildings which have been used or held for future expansion and derive a profit therefrom. Such income is not in the ordinary course of business and would be treated differently in the auditor's financial statement; such incidental income is frequently described on financial statements as "Nonrecurring Income" or "Extraordinary Income."

Certain income accounts because of their nature and because of federal income tax treatment require special auditing. These may be grouped generally as follows:

1. Dividends received.
2. Interest.
3. Rents.
4. Royalties.
5. Gains (or losses) from sale of fixed assets and investments.
6. Other miscellaneous income, not in the ordinary course of business, and not included above.

In auditing the accounts of small and medium-sized businesses, it is rather unusual to find dividend income and interest on obligations of the United States and U. S. instrumentalities and local political subdivisions, since most small businesses do not have an excess of cash funds to invest in the securities producing such income. Many small businesses, however, do have interest income.

This is of particular importance if the company is in the financial business where interest income comprises a substantial portion of the total income. The auditor must determine first whether or not such an organization constitutes a personal holding company within the meaning of Internal Revenue Code section 541, reg. 1.541-1. It is not practicable to enter into a complete discussion of the definition of a personal holding company, and reference should be made to the applicable Code section. Generally speaking, however, a personal holding company is one which has not more than five stockholders at any time during the last half of the taxable year who own more than 50 per cent of the outstanding stock, either directly or indirectly; and at least 60 per cent of the adjusted ordinary gross income for the taxable year is personal holding company income. There is an exception, however, for certain finance companies if they meet the tests as to the source or amount of interest income and the amount of loans to stockholders. Also, it is interesting to note that small business investment companies are excluded from this section. [Internal Revenue Code, sec. 542 (c).]

In this connection, it should be noted that certain elements of income which are income for corporate purposes are not considered income for federal income tax purposes. One example of this is life insurance proceeds received by reason of the death of the insured. Capital gains are given special tax treatment. If the corporation is qualified as a "Small Business Corporation" ("Subchapter S corporation"), income is treated on the federal income tax return in a manner similar to that of a partnership return. In order to properly prepare the return, therefore, attention must be given to segregating and verifying the specific income items during the course of the audit.

AUDIT PROGRAM

Subsequent to Audit Date

1. Review the method of classifying the income accounts.

    Note: *The extent of the work required in this area will depend to a large extent on the system of internal control. Unfortunately, many small business organizations do not have a written accounting manual, and, therefore, the auditor must exercise considerable judgment in determining whether or not the accounts have been properly and adequately journalized during the year. Inconsistency in journalizing will often be found to be the rule, rather than the exception, in auditing small businesses.*

2. A list should be prepared of all income accounts which require special analysis.

    Note: *Following is a useful checklist of those income accounts usually requiring special attention:*

    - Dividends.
    - Interest.
    - Rents.
    - Royalties.
    - Gains from sale of fixed assets.
    - Gains from sale of securities, and/or other investments.
    - Sale of scrap (if treated as an income account).
    - "Miscellaneous" and "Other" income.
    - Cash discounts received (if treated as income account).
    - Commissions (unless a part of regular income).
    - Receipts from life insurance policies.
    - Receipts from casualty insurance policies.
    - Recoveries of bad debts previously charged off.

3. An analysis should be made of each income account which is to be separately shown on the federal income tax return, or on the financial statements, or which for reasons of internal control needs to be investigated.

4. Determine whether or not the income qualifies the corporation as a personal holding company.

    Note: *Personal holding income in excess of allowed amounts will disqualify a "Small Business Corporation."*

5. Prepare and post any necessary adjusting journal entries.

WORKING PAPERS REQUIRED

Dividends

Prepare work sheet showing the date and amount of all dividends received. In the event that there should be a very large number of different dividends, a summary would be satisfactory.

Interest

Prepare a work sheet showing the summary of all interest received, listed by source. Figure 13-1 illustrates one method in which this may be shown so that all of the information necessary for preparation of the federal income tax return will be readily available.

Rents

A work sheet should be prepared showing the total amount of rent received, the amount of depreciation, and other expenses charged against rental income. It will be necessary to make up a work sheet so that all of the information necessary for the federal income tax return can be prepared.

Royalties

A work sheet should be prepared showing the source and amount of all royalties received during the year.

Gains and Losses

The information necessary for this can be obtained from the working papers for fixed assets. Accordingly, no additional work sheets would be necessary unless the asset disposed of is other than "fixed assets." Ordinarily all gains or losses from the sale of assets will fall under the Fixed Asset section, see Chapter 8.

Other Income

It will be necessary to prepare a work sheet for each general ledger account for other income should there be more than one.

METHOD OF VERIFICATION

Verification will fall into one of two categories:

1. Transactions arising from internal sources.
2. Transactions arising from external sources.

XYZ Company
Interest Earned Year Ended
9-30-19XX

ACCT NO		ORDINARY INTEREST	U.S. INTEREST	EXEMPT INTEREST	TOTAL
901	CUSTOMERS' NOTES	500 00			500 00
902	EMPLOYEES' NOTES	200 00			200 00
903	1ST NATIONAL BANK - CERT. OF DEPOSIT	800 00			800 00
906	U.S. 4S 88-93		800 00		800 00
908	STATE OF ILLINOIS GENERAL OBLIGATION 3½S 95			350 00	350 00
		1,500 00	800 00	350 00	2650 00

Figure 13-1

An example of category 1 would be interest which is charged to customers in the normal course of business, and which would normally be evidenced by the preparation of an invoice or other charge document. These are verified by examining copies of the invoices, checking them with the customer's detail ledger account, and verifying that the amounts have been paid by the customer. The extent to which these should be verified in the books will depend to a considerable degree on the internal control system. The auditor should be alert to watch for charges of this nature which have been overlooked by the client's accounting staff.

A common income account is cash discounts received. This has been a subject of some controversy for a number of years between accountants as to whether this constitutes income or whether it constitutes a reduction in cost of sales. There are valid arguments to support both positions. The financial managers are inclined to want to treat it as "Financial Income" which is available to the company because of the fact that its financial planning is such as to permit taking advantage of all cash discounts offered.

On the other hand, the production staff is usually inclined to show it as a reduction in the purchase price of raw material or merchandise. It is probably not too important which way it is treated by the client, provided that the treatment is consistent from year to year. In this connection, the general consensus of opinion is that amounts up to 2 per cent can properly be treated as cash discounts received, but that amounts in excess of 2 per cent should be treated as trade discounts and as a reduction in cost of sales rather than financial income. However, some industries traditionally give additional cash discount of more than 2 per cent for early payment, frequently referred to as "anticipation," and in this case it is properly picked up as financial income, if this is the policy of the client.

An example of category 2 would include such items as interest from notes, bonds, and other interest-bearing securities, including certificates of deposit, short-term government notes and bills, and similar instruments. Dividends are occasionally received from stock held by the corporation as an investment, and a third example would be amounts received from the sale of fixed assets. Each of the external income amounts must be verified by reference to the instrument or the transaction giving rise to the income.

Following are specific areas and the method of verification for each:

Dividends

Dividends are verified by reference to the work sheet prepared when the securities are counted. By reference to standard reports of dividends paid, the amount of the dividends which should have been received can be checked against the amount actually received as shown by the cash receipts book. If any discrepancy should exist, it will be necessary to reconcile the amount.

Note: *Due consideration must be given to ex-dividend dates in determining whether or not a dividend should have been received.*

Interest

The amount of interest received can easily be verified by reference to the securities which give rise to the interest payments. Reference should also be made to the schedule of receivables which will list any notes receivable, the most common form of security giving rise to interest. A schedule should be made up showing the amount of interest which should have been received and this schedule compared with the cash receipts book as to the amount actually received, together with any amounts accrued at the audit date. Any differences should be resolved.

> **Note:** *In many cases, interest-bearing notes given by customers in lieu of accounts payable are often waived as to the interest. There should be some documentary evidence, such as notation in minutes of the director's meetings, or written memorandum by a senior officer authorizing such waiver of interest. In the absence of any such written evidence, the auditor should verify with an appropriate officer that such interest has in fact been waived if such is the case. In the event that a discrepancy does exist between the amount shown as having been due and the amount reported to have been received, the auditor should correspond directly with the payor to determine the amount actually paid.*

Rents

Rents are verified by reference to the lease or other rental agreement. All rents which should have been received should be checked against the amounts reported as received and any differences resolved. If a partnership or an individual federal income tax return is to be filed, the amount of depreciation and other direct expenses should be noted on the work sheet so that the proper federal income tax returns can be filed. On the corporation income tax form 1120 there is no special schedule for net rental income, the income being shown in the gross income section and the deductions being taken in the deductions section under the regular categories.

Royalties

In the event that the company is receiving any royalties, reference would be made to the royalty agreement or such other instrument as may give rise to royalty payments. Royalties should be verified by direct correspondence with the payor thereof.

Net Gains and Losses

Net gains and losses will usually be available from the audit of fixed assets. In the event that there should be a gain or loss on the sale of some asset, not carried in fixed assets, the verification would follow the same procedure as set up in Chapter 8.

Other Income

Each major item of other income should be traced to the cash receipts journal or such other journal of original entry. One common source of other income is cash discounts received. Ordinarily these originate in the cash disbursements journal and a spot check should be made to determine that the amount of discount taken is correct. In this connection, the auditor can be of service to his client if in his review of accounts payable he will make a note of invoices unpaid at the audit date on which cash discounts were available and by his subsequent examination found that the discounts were not taken. In many lines of businesses, the cash discount is great enough to more than pay the cost of borrowing, and at the same time will result in a much better credit rating for the client. While it is not always possible for a client to operate in this manner, the auditor should be aware of the situation and be prepared to advise his client accordingly.

During the analysis of other income, any transaction which has been credited to other income which is properly a reduction of some expense, should be reclassified. For example, freight claims are sometimes found in the "other income" account. These should be reclassified to purchases or some similar account or if the account actually affected is an expense account they should be credited direct to that expense account. In other instances, scrap is sold. If this is general scrap arising merely from the cleaning out of the place of business it probably cannot be properly assigned to any other category. However, if the company consistently produces scrap from a manufacturing operation, the manufacturing operation, "cost of material used," should be credited with scrap sales.

REQUIREMENTS OF SPECIAL SITUATIONS

While even the smallest business organizations usually have an adequate internal control system for recording the routine sales invoices or other regular sales receipts, many provide little or no control over the incidental income items. It is impossible to list all of the items and situations which might conceivably be encountered in auditing small and medium-sized organizations, but the following list is indicative of those areas which justify the auditor's attention:

1. Discounts on sale of merchandise to employees.
2. Recoveries of bad debts.
3. Interest charged to customers and/or employees.
4. Repayment of employees' advances.
5. Sale of incidental supplies.
6. Sale of scrap.

In the case of manufacturing companies, the sale of scrap often assumes substantial proportions. This is an item which is very difficult to control both from the standpoint of internal control and from that of the independent auditor. There have been numerous occasions where companies have suffered financial loss through the fraudulent sale of scrap, usually involving a conspiracy. While the system of internal control will influence the degree of verification necessary, the auditor should be very alert to watch for any evidence which might lead to discovery of improper handling of scrap sales.

Occasionally, a company which is not normally in the business of renting equipment will rent out certain of its facilities, either equipment or premises, and the auditor should verify that if such a transaction occurs a proper charge is made and subsequently collected.

Another area which experience has shown to be susceptible to fraudulent practices is the recovery of bad debts previously charged off. Since these accounts are not on the books at the audit date as assets, they are not ordinarily verified by direct correspondence with the debtor. If collection effort is made by employees of the client, it is good practice to send a routine confirmation request. If the debtor has paid the account but has not received credit for it, he will usually be most prompt in letting the auditor know. If accounts are turned over to a collection agency or attorney, all correspondence should be carefully reviewed. If such records fail to list an account that should have been turned over, it should be investigated. If the volume justifies, the attorney or collection agency should be asked for direct confirmation of the accounts paid during the year and those held for collection at the audit date.

Merchandising firms selling consumer goods traditionally permit employees to purchase goods at a discount. The internal control system will indicate the degree of checking required, but the auditor should analyze the account to see that it appears normal for the volume involved.

FINANCIAL STATEMENT PRESENTATION

Over the years, the statement of profit and loss has undergone a number of changes in title. At present the following are those most commonly used:

- Statement of Income.
- Statement of Income and Expense.
- Statement of Revenue and Expense.
- Statement of Earnings.
- Results of Operations.

  Note: *If the statements represent a consolidation of two or more corporations, the title would be preceded by the word "Consolidated," for example "Consolidated Statement of Earnings."*

The exact caption used is subject to the auditor's judgement. There is a good deal to be said, however, for consistency from year to year in titling the statements for a particular client.

The proper presentation of income on the profit and loss statement will follow the form best adapted to present clearly the operating results for the particular business involved. It is not practicable to list all of the possible ways in which the income account may reasonably be presented. Generally speaking, there should be sufficient detail of the income so that the reader of the financial statements can make his own analysis as to the income received from various aspects of a business. A company operating two or three divisions would by preference show the sales for each. At the same time in order to arrive at a gross profit ratio for each division, the cost of goods sold would be shown as a deduction from the sales for that particular division.

Normal income, which would be "Sales" for a manufacturing or mercantile firm, or "Revenue" for a service organization, is usually stated first on the Statement of Income. It is preferable to show gross sales, and to show sales returns and allowances as a deduction therefrom to arrive at net sales. However, when sales returns and allowances are immaterial, it is satisfactory to show net sales only. Cost of goods sold is deducted from net sales to arrive at gross profit. In the case of a service organization, there is usually no "cost of goods sold" as such, since the costs are made up of all of the general expenses rather than the cost of specific material.

In addition to gross profit from sale of merchandise, manufacturing and mercantile firms may derive profit from commissions on sale of merchandise, rental of equipment, and other items representing essentially compensation for services rather than the sale of merchandise. These items of income should be separately stated so that the ratio of sales to cost of sales is not distorted. This may be presented as follows:

Sales of merchandise		$500,000
Less: Cost of sales		400,000
		100,000
Received from rent of equipment	$5,000	
Customers' service charges	1,000	
Commissions received	4,000	10,000
Total		$110,000

"Other Income" is customarily shown at the bottom of the Statement of Income, and if there are any nonrecurring (extraordinary) items of income, they should be shown separately unless the amount is not significant, in which case they may be included in "Other Income." If the amount of nonrecurring income is significant, a statement should be made in "Notes to Financial Statements" showing its effect on income taxes. Following is an example:

Note A: During the year ended September 30, 19xx, the Corporation sold a tract of vacant land which had been purchased originally for the purpose of providing for expansion of Division S, for a total profit, before income taxes, of $200,000 or 50 cents per share. Income taxes on this sale amounted to $50,000 or 12½ cents per share.

While it is somewhat unusual in auditing small and medium-sized businesses to show net income per share, it is sometimes done. If so, the amount per share of ordinary income, the amount per share of nonrecurring or extraordinary income, and the total amount per share, should all be shown. This may be indicated as follows:

Earnings per share, before nonrecurring income	$1.10
Nonrecurring income per share	.50
Total earnings per share	$1.60

14

Auditing
Expense Accounts

A s is the case with the income accounts, the primary purpose for auditing expense accounts is twofold: First, to insure that they are, in fact, expenses, and are properly classified, and, secondly, to secure information required for preparation of the various income tax returns.

Normal expenses of small and medium-sized businesses can usually be broken down into the following categories:

1. Cost of goods sold.
2. Selling expense.
3. Administrative expense.

   Note: *"Administrative" expense often includes "general expense." "General expense" is usually considered to be such items as interest, auditing and legal fees, and similar items which cannot conveniently be allocated to a particular department or activity.*

Obviously, the specific expense accounts found in an audit will vary widely, dependent upon the type of business. Manufacturing concerns will have many accounts involved in their cost of goods sold, most of which will be incorporated into the cost system. In such a manufacturing business, the cost system may vary from a highly sophisticated to an extremely simple one. The auditor is faced with the problem of determining the adequacy of the cost under these circumstances, since he must value the ending inventory accordingly. This is treated in greater detail in Chapter 6.

In small organizations it will frequently be found that there is no distinction between sales expense and general and administrative expense. The lack of distinction in such cases is not too important. Certain expenses must be reported separately on the federal income tax return and accordingly the auditor should be aware of the accounts falling into this category. Likewise, certain accounts require careful verification to satisfy the requirements of the audit.

For service organizations such as brokers, commission merchants, insurance agencies, hotels, and similar operations, there is ordinarily no cost of goods sold as such. All income is received as fees,. commissions, or rents, and accordingly the cost of sales are the selling, general, and administrative expenses of the operation.

Following is a brief summary of the expenses commonly found in auditing small and medium-sized businesses which require the attention of the auditor.

Labor

For convenience, labor expense is considered to be all sums paid as salaries, wages, commissions, and any other compensation to persons who are determined to be employees for purposes of the Federal Insurance Contributions Act, and who are subject to federal income tax withholding under the Internal Revenue Code. Since wages paid have a direct bearing not only upon the expenses of operation but also upon payroll taxes and insurance, it is highly desirable to prepare a payroll summary. The source of this summary will depend upon the bookkeeping system employed by the client, but usually it can be most conveniently taken directly off of the payroll records. The use of such a summary permits the auditor to check quickly and easily the accrual of the various payroll tax accounts and accrued payroll expense, as well as to trace labor costs into the expense accounts for the period under review. Figure 14-1 shows a suggested summary, which would necessarily be modified to reflect payment on a weekly, biweekly, or some other payroll period (page 182, 183).

Cost of Sales

Cost of sales for a mercantile establishment is determined by taking the opening inventory, which would have been verified during the audit for the previous year, adding net purchases, and subtracting the inventory as of the end of the year, which will have been verified during the current year's audit. The Purchase Journal should be spot-checked to determine that a reasonable procedure has been followed in making entries during the year. This is discussed in more detail in Chapter 3. Freight-in is charged directly to the purchases account by some bookkeepers and others set it up in a separate account. In either case, it is essential to see that incoming freight cost is included in cost of goods sold. In the case of a manufacturing concern, the cost of goods sold normally will develop from the cost accounting system in use. This has been discussed in detail in Chapter 6.

Selling expense is usually considered to include sales salaries and commissions, payroll taxes and insurance thereon, travel of sales personnel, entertainment of customers, advertising, including such items as catalogs, mailing lists, printing of advertising material, and maintenance of an advertising department, if such is maintained. In some instances, it will be found that the cost of maintaining the clerical staff handling sales inquiries is also charged to selling expense. In addition delivery expense is often considered as a selling expense, although this will vary from client to client. The more important elements of selling expenses are discussed in detail as follows:

Commissions

Commissions may be paid to either employees or to independent contractors, or to both. The auditor should be alert for payments as commissions which might be interpreted to be paid to employees. The importance of this is that at some later date upon an income tax examination, such commission may be ruled to be subject to payroll taxes and federal income tax withholding. Failure to set up such commissions properly as salaries and withhold the required taxes may result in a deficiency tax, and thus additional liability. It is important, therefore, that the client be aware of any potential tax liability in this area. The auditor must satisfy himself that all commissions paid to independent contractors are bona fide and are not subject to payroll taxes and to income tax withholding.

Travel and Entertainment Expense

The Internal Revenue Code imposes strict requirements for the reporting and deducting of travel and entertainment expenses. These are too lengthy to be quoted in detail, but the auditor should be familiar with such requirements. One of the essential requirements is that if a payment to an employee as reimbursement of travel and/or entertainment expense is to be deducted by the employer and not be taxable to the employee, that proper records be maintained. Generally speaking, these require that each expense report show the date and time of the entertainment, name of customer and the company represented, where the entertainment took place, and what subject was discussed. While these expense reports do not have to be prepared daily, they must be based upon a diary maintained by the employee claiming the reimbursement and the diary must be kept on an acceptable basis, which usually means that it must be entered at the time or close to the time that the expense is incurred. Certain items of travel expense must be evidenced by receipts. These include all expense for lodging, transportation by public carrier, items of food, and entertainment over $25. It is interesting to note that in this connection credit card charges are not in themselves sufficient evidence, although they do provide verification of the amount charged. Insofar as the Internal Revenue Service is concerned, the use of credit cards is no different than the payment of cash. Gifts are frequently made to customers, particularly on the occasion of holidays, and such are properly deductible provided they do not exceed $25 in value, under present regulations. One problem often encountered among smaller clients is that of a travel advance having been made to an officer of the company and no accounting subsequently provided. This may result in a disallowance of the expense, at least so far as the employee is concerned, who may find that he is required to pay personal tax on additional income represented by the unaccounted for travel advance.

XYZ Company
Payroll Summary
Year Ended 9-30-19XX

| Payroll Period Ended: | Gross Payroll | WITHHELD | | | |
		FICA	Federal Income Tax	State Income Tax	Insurance
October 3	384000	11400	50000	3800	10000
10	409000	12200	58000	4100	10000
17	412000	12500	62000	4100	11000
24	429000	13000	70000	4300	12000
31	413000	12900	60000	4100	11000
	2047000	62000	300000	20400	54000
Less: Accrued 10-1-XW	87000				
	1960000				
Add: Accrued 10-31-XW	140000				
Total Expense	2100000				
November 7	409000	12200	58000	4100	10000
14	429000	13000	70000	4300	12000
21	460000	15000	78000	4600	13000
Total-Year-Cash Basis	29210000	1210000	3780000	292000	638000
Accrued: 10-1-XW —	87000				
Accrued: 9-30-XX +	138000				
	29261000				

Figure 14-1

EXPENSE DISTRIBUTION

NET PAYROLL	OFFICERS' SALARIES	OFFICE SALARIES	SALES SALARIES	SUPERVISION	DIRECT LABOR	REPAIR	DELIVERY
308800	50000	40000	40000	25000	185000	29000	15000
324700	50000	40000	48000	25000	210000	21000	15000
322400	50000	40000	45000	25000	213000	24000	15000
329700	50000	40000	42000	25000	226000	31000	15000
325000	50000	40000	45000	25000	206000	32000	15000
1610600	250000	200000	220000	125000	1040000	137000	75000
	10000	15000	10000	5000	40000	5000	2000
	240000	185000	210000	120000	1000000	132000	73000
	15000	20000	20000	10000	60000	8000	7000
	255000	205000	230000	130000	1060000	140000	80000
324700	50000	40000	48000	25000	210000	21000	15000
329700	50000	40000	42000	25000	226000	31000	15000
349400	50000	50000	51000	25000	244000	25000	15000
23290000	3000000	3150000	5190000	1590000	13760000	1710000	810000
	10000	15000	10000	5000	40000	5000	2000
	10000	18000	18000	7000	73000	9000	3000
	3000000	3153000	5198000	1592000	13793000	1714000	811000

Figure 14-1 (contd.)

Advertising

Advertising expense is often a major item of cost of operations. It will frequently be found that not all advertising expenditures are charged to the advertising account. For example, nearly every business advertises in the telephone directory, and these charges are usually added to the monthly telephone bill. When paid, the entire telephone bill is charged to "telephone" expense, rather than distributed between advertising and telephone expense. If the amount of the advertising portion is small, it is not important. However, it is not unusual to find that the advertising portion is more than half of the entire monthly telephone charge. The cost of printing brochures and other advertising material, including the mailing envelopes or folders and postage is properly chargeable to advertising expense, although it often ends up in "office supplies." Where the amounts are at all substantial, the auditor will do his client a great favor by properly reclassifying advertising costs. The corporation federal income tax return requires that the amount of advertising be shown as a separate item.

Administrative expenses may be regarded as all of those expenses not considered under one of the foregoing categories. Following are those most commonly encountered.

Taxes

From an auditing viewpoint, taxes are a troublesome area that merits careful attention because of the penalty imposed for failure to report and pay on time. Especially among smaller businessmen who do not usually have experienced tax personnel on their staff, the auditor has to be particularly careful that all required taxes have been reported and paid. Taxes may be generally categorized as follows:

- Payroll taxes.
- Sales and use taxes.
- Licenses, permits, fees, etc.
- Property taxes.
- Income taxes.

Under payroll taxes will be found the employer's portion of the federal insurance contribution act taxes (FICA), state, and federal unemployment taxes. In some jurisdictions where the state operates the workmen's compensation plan, the premiums paid to state agencies are often considered as a tax. It is immaterial whether this is recorded as a tax or treated as insurance expense, since it constitutes ordinary business expense in any case. Consistency is a virtue and, therefore, if the client has customarily included premiums paid to the state for workingmen's compensation insurance as "taxes," it may well be continued in this category.

Sales and use taxes are state or local in nature, so that it is not practicable to attempt to list all of those that might apply in a given circumstance. It is assumed that the auditor is familiar with those that apply to his locality, and can conduct his audit accordingly.

Likewise, most licenses, permits, and fees are local in nature, although there are a few which are federal, for example narcotics permits required of doctors and druggists, fees on heavy trucks, licenses for dealers in firearms, etc. These are often treated as expenses in the category in which incurred, rather than taxes. For example, automobile and truck licenses are often charged to auto and truck expense. Licenses to engage in business, such as occupational licenses are often charged to sales or to general expense. Again, since in any event they constitute ordinary and necessary business expenses and are minor in amount, it is probably not too important whether they be treated as business expenses or as taxes.

Property taxes ordinarily are those imposed by state and local governments on real estate and personal property. Even though a client does not own real estate, he will almost certainly have incurred a liability for taxes on personal property.

In the area of income taxes, however, a completely different situation is encountered. It is extremely important that all income taxes be segregated by type, that is, whether federal, state, or local government, as the deductibility and the accounting treatment of income taxes is quite distinct from ordinary business operating taxes. It is assumed that the accountant is familiar with the requirements of the Internal Revenue Code as to the preparation of federal income tax returns and with the requirements for any state and local income taxes which may be required.

Rent

Rent is an item which is required to be reported as a separate item on federal income tax returns. While it is proper to include incidental rental of equipment in this category, more often the expense is simply left in the account to which it was originally charged. Rents paid for the rental of real property, however, should be segregated and recorded on the income tax return as such.

Bad Debt Expense

Special information is required for bad debt expense if the client is on a reserve basis, and in any event the amount is required to be shown separately on the federal income tax return. This subject is discussed in detail in Chapter 5.

Repairs

Ordinarily the cost of repairs may be distributed over several different accounts. For federal income tax return purposes, however, it is necessary to segregate the repairs and show them as one total. In this regard, the auditor must be careful to see that the repairs are properly maintenance and repair charges and are not capitalizable items.

Interest

In addition to being a separate item in the income tax return, interest expense is of particular importance to the auditor since it originates with a liability which must be verified. This is discussed fully in Chapter 9.

Contributions

The auditor of small and medium-sized businesses often finds a variety of expenditures charged to the contributions account. Some may be unallowable for tax purposes, and some may simply be misclassified. Many managers are unaware of the percentage limitations for allowable deductions on the federal (and usually state) income tax returns, and may be quite surprised to find that there is a tax deduction loss. While the unused portion of the contribution expense can be carried forward to future years to a limited extent, the client should be made aware of the situation so that it can be avoided in the future.

Depreciation Amortization Depletion

Depreciation is found in virtually all audits, and occasionally amortization. Both of these items of expenses are discussed in detail in Chapter 8. Depletion will be found if the business involves mining, oil, or gas production. Each of these expenses are required to be shown separately on the federal income tax return.

AUDIT PROGRAM

Subsequent to Audit Date

1. Prepare a list of all expense accounts which are to be analyzed and/or scrutinized.

   Note: *Since many of the expense accounts are coordinated with the analysis of the related liability or asset account, a notation should be made on the list if a separate work sheet will not be required.*

2. Prepare work sheets as required.

3. Prepare and post any necessary adjusting journal entries.

WORKING PAPERS REQUIRED

While it is not possible to give an all-inclusive list of expense accounts for which working papers will be needed, the following is a representative list of those most frequently encountered and which for audit and/or tax purposes will need to be analyzed:

1. Officer's Salaries.

   Note: *This information may be available from the analysis of payroll. Since this is an item which must be reported separately for federal income tax purposes,* *it is necessary to prepare a work sheet showing for each officer the total compensation paid during the year, the officer's address and social security number, and the amount of expense allowances, if any. If the salary of the officer plus expense allowance is less than $10,000, it is not necessary to complete the expense account column.*

2. Repairs.

   Note: *The principal reason for an analysis of repair accounts is to insure that no items which should have been capitalized are expensed through the repair account.*

3. Bad Debts.

   Note: *This account will probably have been analyzed in the auditing of accounts receivable as outlined in Chapter 5.*

4. Rents.

   Note: *In this account, as stated earlier, it will frequently be found that the rental of equipment will be charged to the section, department, cost center, or activity in which it is used, rather than to a general rent expense account. Rental of office equipment, for example, will be charged to "office expense." Likewise, it is rather common for businesses to lease automobiles and trucks, and the cost of these leases is often charged to the departmental expense account. There is some question as to whether it is proper income tax procedure to include rents for equipment as "rents" on the income tax return, but there is no question that rents paid for the use of land and buildings should be included in this category.*

5. Interest.

   Note: *An analysis of all interest payments will be required. It will usually not be necessary to prepare additional work papers, as the information will have been made in preparing the Notes Payable work papers as described in Chapter 9.*

6. Contributions.

   Note: *A detailed list of charitable contributions must be prepared. In reviewing this, it is important to ascertain that all of the amounts claimed as contributions, are, in fact, allowable contributions; that is, that they conform to the Internal Revenue Code definition of allowable contributions. Generally speaking, a deductible contribution is one made to an organization which itself is tax exempt. If there is any question, reference should be made to the Internal Revenue Service for a ruling.*

7. Depreciation and Amortization.

   Note: *Depreciation and amortization will ordinarily be audited with Fixed Assets as outlined in Chapter 8. One exception, often encountered, is the amortization of organization expense which is treated in Chapter 7.*

8. Advertising.

   Note: *One situation that often will be noted in auditing the advertising accounts is the tendency to put certain items which actually constitute contributions in the advertising expense account. This will include such things as advertising in fraternal magazines, charitable programs, and the like, which are more in the nature of a donation. However, so long as the client's name is actually shown,* *it would appear that it is proper to charge it to advertising. The auditor should watch for charges of tickets to various types of charitable entertainment to this account, since upon examination, Internal Revenue agents will usually disallow the deduction as advertising expense. An exception would probably be in the case of a company buying season tickets or a large block of tickets to various sporting events with the purpose of distributing them to customers. This is a normal and legitimate activity, although there may be some question as to whether or not it is more properly treated as entertainment expense.*

9. Entertainment.

Note: *Perhaps the most important thing to be observed in the entertainment expense accounts is to insure that all reimbursement of officers and employees has been made in accordance with the established procedure. It is particularly important to insure that the procedure for the approval of such expense accounts is in accordance with the applicable regulations of the Internal Revenue Code. Failure to do so can result in a disallowance to the corporation and subsequent additional taxation of the amounts to the recipient. Entertainment expenses allowed to officers and stockholders should especially be scrutinized. The auditor should also satisfy himself that any charges to entertainment come within the activities permitted by the applicable Internal Revenue Code sections.*

10. Insurance.

Note: *The insurance expense account is usually audited in connection with the audit of the Prepaid Insurance account and is covered in detail in Chapter 7.*

11. Taxes.

Note: *If desired, the work papers for taxes can be combined with the work papers for accrued taxes as described in Chapter 12. Such a consolidation saves considerable time since the information is the same for both. As explained in Chapter 12, work sheets will be required for the following:*

> *1. Payroll taxes.*
>
> *2. Sales and use taxes.*
>
> *3. Licenses, permits, fees, etc.*
>
> *4. Property taxes.*
>
> *5. Income taxes.*

12. Depletion.

Note: *Depletion will ordinarily be encountered only in those businesses dealing with mining, quarrying, and oil and gas production. This is a most important item of expense for those companies affected, since it involves not only an expense but an important tax deduction.*

13. Casualty and Theft Losses.

Note: *Well-run businesses will usually insure against the more common perils, so that in the event of a loss the auditor will need to check the insurance coverage (if any), to determine the amount of the actual loss.*

14. Professional Fees.

Note: *This expense account will often be captioned "Legal and Auditing" or some similar title. Analysis of this account is particularly significant, since it will reveal the names of all attorneys who have been employed during the year. All such attorneys should be sent requests for information as described in Chapter 1. Payments to consultants may indicate various plans in progress which must be analyzed to determine that all liability in connection therewith has been reflected on the books.*

15. Miscellaneous.

Note: *Miscellaneous expense accounts, which may be called "Other," "General," or by some similar name, must be analyzed to determine their contents, which often will require reclassification.*

16. Extraordinary and Nonrecurring Expenses.

Note: *Nonrecurring expenses should be verified according to their nature, and might consist of additional income or other tax assessments, loss on sale of assets, losses by theft, fire, or other casualty not covered by insurance. Some may have been audited in one or more of the foregoing expense classifications. If the amount is material, it should be segregated.*

METHOD OF VERIFICATION

Verification can usually be made by reference to invoices, contracts, and similar documents. Since many of the expense accounts will have been audited in connection with the associated asset or liability, only those accounts not so verified would require additional procedures.

REQUIREMENTS OF SPECIAL SITUATIONS

Comparison of expense accounts from one year to the next, both by type and by amount will point out areas that justify further investigation. For example, a sudden increase in legal expense from one year to the next, would be reason for the auditor to question additional liability, either actual or potential, from lawsuits. Similarly, any sudden decrease in an expense account would make the auditor question whether or not an expense had been omitted on the books, or was perhaps misclassified. The auditor should be constantly alert for any expense accounts which do not appear reasonable to the business being conducted.

FINANCIAL STATEMENT PRESENTATION

As is the case with the income accounts, the object of the financial presentation of the expense accounts is to be as informative as possible. The common method of presenting the statements is to show the cost of sales deducted from net sales, preferably for each department, division, etc. Selling expense can often be segregated also by department, division, etc. When this can be done, it provides maximum information for the reader.

General and administrative expenses, by their nature, can be shown only for the operation as a whole. If there are any extraordinary or nonrecurring expenses that are material in amount, they should be shown separately as the last item before income taxes. If such nonrecurring expense results in a lower income tax than would otherwise have been paid, the amount should be shown, either on the statement itself or as a "Note to Financial Statements." Following is one way this situation may be presented:

Net profit before nonrecurring expense and income taxes	$100,000
Nonrecurring loss on sale of factory property	25,000
Net profit before income taxes	75,000
Federal and state income taxes—Note A	30,000
Net profit for year	$ 45,000

Note A: Income taxes for the year would have been approximately $12,500 greater if it had not been for the loss incurred on the sale of land and buildings formerly used for a factory.

15

The Auditor's Opinion

The standards of reporting [1] are as follows:

1. The report shall state whether the financial statements are presented in accordance with generally accepted principles of accounting.
2. The report shall state whether such principles have been consistently observed in the current period in relation to the preceding period.
3. Informative disclosures in the financial statement are to be regarded as reasonably adequate, unless otherwise stated in the report.
4. The report shall either contain an expression of opinion regarding the financial statements, taken as a whole, or an assertion to the effect that an opinion cannot be expressed. When an overall opinion cannot be expressed, the reasons therefor should be stated. In all cases where an auditor's name is associated with financial statements, the report shall contain a clear-cut indication of the character of the auditor's examination, if any, and the degree of responsibility he is taking.

The first standard states that "the report shall state whether the financial statements are presented in accordance with generally accepted principles of accounting." One of the thornier problems facing the accounting profession is an acceptable definition of "generally accepted principles of accounting." Many attempts have been made to define these principles. Obviously, they are based upon a broad spectrum of accounting writing and experience. Certainly, to be acceptable under the definition of the first

---

[1] "Statements on Auditing Procedure #33," Auditing Standards and Procedures, American Institute of Certified Public Accountants, New York.

standard of reporting, the principles must be in general use in the industry or business being audited. Fortunately for the auditor of small and medium-sized businesses, he is usually spared some of the more complex problems such as pooling of interest and consolidation of foreign subsidiaries.

Generally accepted principles of accounting are expounded in numerous textbooks, reference books, and publications. Probably the most authoritative is represented by the "Opinions of the Accounting Principles Board," of the American Institute of Certified Public Accountants.[2] These publications represent the consensus of opinion of Certified Public Accountants in the United States. The auditor must be mindful of the fact that accounting principles evolve just as do all other factors in economic life. Current "Opinions" are issued to reflect the changing of acceptance of accounting principles.

The second standard of reporting states that "the report shall show whether or not such principles have been consistently observed." In other words, there is not only the factor of determining "generally accepted principles of accounting" but also the determination of whether or not the client has consistently observed these principles in his accounting. Accordingly, the auditor must in effect combine the first two standards, determining first, that the statements of the client are in accordance with generally accepted accounting principles, and secondly, that these principles have been consistently applied. A common example of inconsistency among small and medium-sized businesses is the method of determining quantities and valuation of inventories from one fiscal period to the next. A second example is the change from a write-off to a reserve method for treating bad debts. A third would be the setting up of reserves for such expenses as warranties, vacations, and other costs.

As in all judgements, the auditor must take into consideration the materiality of the items, should he find them treated inconsistently. If the amount is not significant, certainly the auditor would not find it necessary to take exception in his opinion. However, any inconsistency in the client's accounting records from one period to another regardless of size, should be called to the attention of the client. Many of these occur inadvertently, and upon notification, will be corrected by the client.

The third standard of reporting states that the "informative disclosures in the financial statements are to be regarded as reasonably adequate unless otherwise stated in the report." Unless specifically stated to the contrary, the reader is entitled to rely upon the statements as being complete and factual. This standard of reporting does not intend or presume to dictate the specific wording, but it does state that whatever wording is used must be clear and complete, or if not complete, then full disclosure must be made.

Disclosure may be made in footnotes to financial statements, on the financial statements themselves, or as a part of the opinion. The exact method of such disclosures will depend upon the significance of the disclosure. In the chapters devoted to specific areas of the audit, under the section on "Financial Statement Presentation" suggestions for making such disclosures have been made.

---

[2] American Institute of Certified Public Accountants, New York.

Wording should be complete, but as concise as the circumstances will permit. Wording must be clear and leave no room for misinterpretation.

In preparing financial statements the auditor must use judgement in determining which accounts are to be consolidated, since to present every item in the general ledger would be merely to copy the trial balance, with the result that the information would be so voluminous as to be of little value. This problem is discussed in detail in the chapters covering the various specific audit areas.

The fourth standard of reporting concerns the opinion. In this regard the word "opinion" is used in a limited sense, referring to the opinion paragraph only; whereas, the term "opinion" in its broad meaning is commonly used to encompass the entire "short form" report. In conformity with the fourth standard, the auditor must issue one of the following:

1. Unqualified opinion.

   Note: *Ideally, all audits should contain an unqualified opinion, which simply means that the auditor is able to express his opinion as to the adequacy and correctness of the financial statements, without exception, in accordance with all of the applicable auditing standards.*

2. Qualified opinion.

   Note: *Inevitably, there will be occasions when it will be necessary to express a qualified opinion, because it is not possible to comply with all of the auditing standards. This may arise as a result of the time that the auditor is engaged to make the audit. For example in the case of an initial audit, the opening inventory, having been taken prior to the time of the engagement, usually cannot be verified, so that it will be necessary to qualify the opinion as it applies to the statement of income. Also, there may be restrictions placed upon the scope of the audit by the client. For example, there may be certain receivables that are not to be directly confirmed. This situation may call for a qualified opinion.*

3. Adverse opinion.

   Note: *An adverse opinion indicates that the financial statements do not present fairly the financial position or results of operations in conformity with generally accepted accounting principles. Since this type of an opinion is most undesirable, the auditor should make every effort to notify his client as early as possible of the likelihood of such a conclusion.*

4. Disclaimer of opinion.

   Note: *In auditing small and medium-sized businesses, the auditor will often find on the occasion of a first audit particularly, that there is simply insufficient evidential matter in the books and records of the client to permit him to express any opinion. In this situation, he must clearly disclaim any opinion.*

In its simplest presentation, the so-called "standard short form report," in addition to the salutation, auditor's signature, and the date, contains two paragraphs, an expository paragraph and the opinion paragraph:

  1. Expository paragraph.

   a. Statements audited.

    1. Balance sheet.

    2. Statement of income.

    3. Statement of retained earnings.

    4. Statement of source and application of funds.

   b. Statement that the examination was made in accordance with generally accepted auditing standards.

  2. Opinion paragraph.

The "standard short form report" usually reads as follows:

Board of Directors
XYZ Corporation
Our Town, State

   We have examined the balance sheet of the

       XYZ CORPORATION

as of September 30, 19xx, and the related statements of income, retained earnings, and source and application of funds for the year then ended. Our examination was made in accordance with generally accepted auditing standards, and accordingly included such tests of the accounting records and such other auditing procedures as we considered necessary under the circumstances.

   In our opinion, the accompanying balance sheet and statement of income, retained earnings, and source and application of funds present fairly the financial position of the XYZ CORPORATION as of September 30, 19xx, and the results of its operations and source and application of funds for the year then ended, in conformity with generally accepted accounting principles applied on a basis consistent with that of the preceding year.

         Able, Baker, and Carr

Our Town, State
December 5, 19xx

While the "standard" report as shown above includes the statement of source and application of funds, this is by no means a universally followed practice, and in the event that this statement is not included with the report, then reference to it would be omitted. However, modern auditing practice is to include it.

Scope

Two situations may limit the scope of the audit. First, there may be circumstances beyond the control of either the client or the auditor; for example, the first audit of a going business. In this case, it would not have been possible for the auditor to observe the physical count of the beginning inventory, and often he will be unable to satisfy himself as to the adequacy of that count. Accordingly, it would be necessary to modify the scope of the examination. Assuming that the remainder of the audit has been satisfactory, the auditor could express a qualified opinion. The expository paragraph would be modified as follows:

. . . . and such other auditing procedures as we considered necessary under the circumstances, except as noted in the following paragraph.

A middle paragraph would then be added:

Because we were not engaged as auditors until after September 30, 19xw, we were not present to observe the physical inventory taken at that date and we have been unable to satisfy ourselves concerning inventory quantities by other procedures. The beginning inventory has a significant effect on the results of operations for the year. Therefore, we do not express an opinion on the accompanying statements of income and retained earnings for the year ended September 30, 19xx.

There are times, however, when the auditor can satisfy himself as to the adequacy of the beginning inventory count. For example, the client may maintain a perpetual inventory system that can be satisfactorily reconciled to the beginning of the year. In this event, the middle paragraph could be written as follows:

Because we were not engaged as auditors until after September 30, 19xw, we were not present to observe the physical inventory taken at that date. We have been able to satisfy ourselves as to the substantial accuracy of the inventory count made at that time by other procedures.

The second situation which may limit the scope of the audit are restrictions imposed by the client. Most commonly the restriction will be on confirming certain receivables. If the amount involved is significant, it may be such as to preclude the auditor's forming any opinion at all. Often, however, they are applied to certain limited items, and if this is the case, the auditor can take exception in his report but still be able to express an opinion.

For example, a client may have rental charges due him which for some reason he does not wish to have confirmed directly with the debtor. Assuming that these do not materially affect the balance sheet or the income statement, the auditor could express his opinion in accordance with the following:

> . . . . and such other auditing procedures as we considered necessary under the circumstances, except as noted in the following paragraph.

The auditor would then add a middle paragraph worded along the following lines:

> In accordance with your instructions, we did not request direct confirmation from customers owing charges for rental of equipment. Accordingly, we do not express an opinion as to accrued rental receivable in the stated amount of $5,000, which amount enters into the determination of financial position and results of operations.

The opinion paragraph would then be modified to read somewhat as follows:

> In our opinion, with the exception stated in the preceding paragraph, the accompanying balance sheet . . . . etc.

Note: *The cardinal point is always: When does an exception become so material as to preclude an opinion? Unfortunately, there is no simple answer, it is always dependent upon the auditor's judgement. One auditor may consider the exception so vital as to exclude an opinion, while his colleague will issue an opinion with appropriate exception.*

In addition to the qualifications cited above, the client may impose such restrictions upon the scope of the audit itself that no opinion can be expressed. The client may decline to make an adequate count of the inventory, and thus preclude the auditor from making any check of the physical quantities. Assuming that the amount of the inventory is material, this situation might be such that the auditor would have to disclaim any opinion. This might be expressed as follows:

Board of Directors
XYZ Corporation
Our Town, State

We have examined the balance sheet of the

XYZ CORPORATION

as of September 30, 19xx, and the related statements of income, retained earnings, and source and application of funds for the year then ended. Our examination was made in accordance with generally accepted auditing standards and accordingly included such tests of the accounting records and such other auditing procedures as we considered necessary under the circumstances, except as explained in the following paragraph.

No physical count was made of the inventory on hand at September 30, 19xx, so that we were unable to observe the inventory count nor were we able to make any other satisfactory tests of the quantities on hand at that date.

Since the value of the inventory represents a material amount of the assets at September 30, 19xx, we are unable to express an opinion on the accompanying financial statements.

Able, Baker, and Carr

Our Town, State
December 5, 19xx

In the above situation, the auditor may feel that he has satisfactorily audited other areas of the financial statements so that he is able to express an opinion on these particular areas. For example, he may have made an adequate examination of the accounts receivable so that an opinion could be expressed. The danger in doing this, however, is that such a limited expression of opinion may be interpreted by a reader to mean that the entire financial statements have been satisfactorily audited, and thus that the opinion is unqualified.

Subsequent Events

Many auditing procedures are completed subsequent to the audit date. Any event taking place during this period which materially affects the financial statements must be taken into consideration by the auditor. One example would be the failure to collect a large account receivable. Another might be the filing of a lawsuit against the client.

In addition to the foregoing, an event may occur subsequent to the delivery of the audit report, which, if known earlier, would have necessitated a qualified opinion, or even an adverse opinion. Under these circumstances, the auditor may find it necessary to withdraw his opinion. If this is done, the auditor is under an obligation to notify not only the client, but also any third parties of whom the auditor has knowledge, including the SEC if the audit report has been filed there.

Unaudited Statements

The auditor is frequently requested to prepare financial statements from the books without audit. Interim statements, for example, are often prepared. In such instances, the responsibility assumed by the auditor must be clearly indicated. The following wording is often used:

> The foregoing financial statements have been prepared from the books without audit or independent verification, and no accountant's opinion is supplied or intended.

For interim statements, when the auditor normally performs an annual audit, the following wording is appropriate:

> The above interim financial statements have been prepared from the books without independent verification, are subject to final audit, and no accountant's opinion is supplied or intended.

Many managers of small and medium-sized businesses are not fully aware of the work involved or the responsibility assumed by the public accountant in performing an audit. Accordingly, they often ask the accountant to prepare financial statements and erroneously refer to these statements as "audits," and may even present them to credit grantors as "audited statements." If the auditor's name appears in connection with such statements in any way, either by having them typed on his stationery, or even by having his name mentioned in connection with them, he must be certain that a full and complete disclaimer appears.

16

The Auditor's Report

The tangible result, from the client's point of view, of all of the work of the auditor, is contained in the final written report. Accordingly, the report must be meticulously prepared, not only from the standpoint of its contents, but its physical appearance. Careless or shabby typing, for example, may well give an impression of careless auditing. The size and format of the stationery and covers used are subject to the auditor's personal preference. However, the material must be of top quality, and the printed format should be conservative if the auditor wishes to impress his client with his own competence.

It seems incredible, but a review of a large number of audit reports of small and medium-sized businesses indicates that the single most common fault is simple arithmetical mistakes. Many of these are undoubtedly the result of typographical errors in transcription, but they do demonstrate the absolute necessity of adequate checking. How can the auditor expect any reader of his report to place confidence in it if the columns don't foot?

With the advent of a practical offset press, suitable for office use, most accountants have turned to this method of reproducing audit reports. If the size of the auditor's office does not justify the expense of such equipment together with a trained operator, it is usually possible to make arrangements with a commercial printer to do this work. If printing audit reports is to be done outside the accountant's office, however, he must insure that such work will be held completely confidential. With increased clerical costs, it is rather rare to produce audit reports in the old manner of typing an original and a number of carbon copies. If only two or three copies are required, one practical method is to type an original and prepare copies on an office copying machine. The electrostatic machines now available produce acceptable copies.

While the design of audit report paper is one of personal preference, the auditor's name and his city address should appear on each sheet of paper used. His complete letterhead may be used for the first page and/or for the letter of transmittal. Also, reasonable precautions should be taken in binding to insure that sheets are not removed and used separately without reference to the remainder of the report; although, admittedly, this is something that the auditor will have little control over once it has left his office. Bindings are also a matter of personal preference. Brass eyelets are the most commonly used, although spiral binding which permits easier opening and reading of the report has come into considerable favor.

One satisfactory method to provide for adequate checking of the report is by the use of a Report Instructions form. This not only provides for adequate checking, but is used to instruct the stenographic department as to what to prepare. Following is an example:

REPORT INSTRUCTIONS

Client:

Partner in charge: *Auditor in charge:*

Type of report:

Audit date: *Date report due:*

Method of reproduction:

Number of copies: *Number to bind:*   *Number for file:*

Special instructions for covers:

Typed by: *Date:*

Proofread by: *Date:*

References cross-checked by: *Date:*

Footings checked by: *Date:*

Final review by: *Date:*

Delivered: *Date:*   *Via:*

When the Report Instructions form is completed, it is filed with the audit work papers. The person making the final review would check for such errors as spelling, misplaced dollar signs, lines (most important in financial statements), and similar items not specifically covered by other checkers, as well as for general appearance.

The first rule of any writing is to have the audience in mind. An audit report is inclined to be written in stereotyped prose. Like legal writing there is a good basis for this, in that such wording has been tested by time and found to be satisfactory. However, the report will be most useful to a client if it is written in language which he can understand. A report might be written in somewhat simple language for a small client, comparatively unsophisticated in financial affairs, and one who has not had much experience in reading and understanding financial statements. A different style could be used if the report is going to a client who is accustomed to analyzing financial statements and is competent to make his own interpretations.

In each chapter, suggestions have been made as to financial statement presentation. The wording used throughout this manual is intended to be illustrative. It would necessarily be modified to suit the specific situation. The report usually starts with a title page which shows the name of the client and the date of the audit. The second page will comprise the opinion, and the remainder of the report will contain the Balance Sheet, the Analysis of Retained Earnings, the Income Statement, and Application of Funds Statement. Following that, if it is to be included, will be the supplemental information.

"Notes to Financial Statements" comprise an integral part of the financial statement presentation, and it is customary to add the wording: "The accompanying Notes to Financial Statements comprise an integral part of these statements," or something similar, on each of the formal financial statements. Many disclosures required by auditing standards can best be made by the use of such "Notes." In each chapter, under the section on "Financial Statement Presentation," indication has been given to material usually included in "Notes."

The opinion and the financial statements have been discussed in detail in previous chapters. The supplemental information section is usually preceded by a statement, of which the following is typical:

> The audited financial statements of the corporation and our report thereon are presented in the preceding section of this report. The financial information presented hereinafter and in the following comments was derived from the accounting records tested by us as part of the auditing procedures followed in our examination of the aforementioned financial statements, and in our opinion it is fairly presented in all material respects in relation to the financial statements taken as a whole.

This statement is usually placed separately on a page just preceding the supplemental information. However, if desired, it could be used as the opening paragraph in a general explanation of the supplemental information. Following this statement a very brief history of the client may be inserted. Such a statement might be as follows:

> The XYZ Company was incorporated under the laws of Our State on October 15, 19zz. It was the successor to a partnership established three years earlier. The company is engaged primarily in the sale of industrial equipment, and its major customers are contractors, city and state governments, and large manufacturers. The company carries a limited inventory of machinery and equipment, but the larger amount of sales are made by direct shipment from the manufacturer to the customer. In addition, the company also acts as a manufacturer's representative for certain principals who bill and ship direct, the company

receiving a commission for such sales. Most of the lines represented are on an exclusive basis for the territory served.

Its principal place of business is West Street, Our Town, State, and in addition, warehouses are maintained in South City and North City, State.

Officers of the corporation are:

John Doe, President
Richard Rowe, Vice-President
John Jones, Treasurer
James Smith, Secretary

Following were stockholders at September 30, 19xx:

	No. of Shares	%
John Doe	600	60
Richard Rowe	200	20
John Jones	200	20

Following the history and organization of the company, the financial analyses should follow. Results of operations are usually of prime importance, and a condensed statement showing certain basic elements is a convenient and useful statement. Comparative statements are nearly always preferable. The following may be taken as an example:

CONDENSED COMPARATIVE STATEMENT OF INCOME

Years Ended September 30, 19xx and 19xw

	Year Ended September 30,			
	19xx		*19xw*	
	Amount	*%*	*Amount*	*%*
Sales	$510,000	102	$445,000	101
Less: Returns and allowances	10,000	2	5,000	1
Net sales	500,000	100	440,000	100
Cost of sales (less depreciation)	375,000	75	330,000	75
	125,000	25	110,000	25
Selling expense	50,000	10	52,800	12
Administrative expense	25,000	5	22,000	5

Net income before income taxes and depreciation	50,000	10	35,200	8
Depreciation	5,000	1	4,400	1
Net income before income taxes	45,000	9	30,800	7
Federal and state income taxes	20,000	4	13,200	3
Net income	$ 25,000	5	$ 17,600	4

In this example, depreciation is illustrated as a separate item in order to show its effect upon income. If it is immaterial, as in the case with many businesses, it would be included with the regular classifications. Any other single item of income or expense, that in the opinion of the auditor merits special attention, can be shown in a similar manner. It is customary to show the current year in the left-hand column, and the prior year in the right-hand column. If desired, three, four, or more years' results can be listed. However, if any of the prior years have not been audited, or if they have been audited by some other accountant, this must be clearly disclosed. If there have been any material changes in method of accounting, the prior years' statements should be restated, and a full disclosure made of the nature and amounts which have been restated. If two or more years' results are shown on a comparative statement, they must always be strictly comparative.

Following the results of operations, it is advisable to insert any comment regarding unusual occurences during the year by which they may have been affected. For example, if the company experienced a strike or if there were a strike at one of its major customers which might have an effect on operations, it would be pertinent to include this information. Following is an example of how this might be presented:

> During the year there was a major strike in the construction industry which lasted for approximately four and one-half months. During this period nearly all basic construction was shut down. For this reason the company sales suffered, since a large segment of its customers made no purchases at all during this period.

Following a statement regarding operations, it is advisable to include comments and summaries of the major items of assets and liabilities. The following paragraphs show how this might be presented:

Cash on Hand and in Banks

Following is a summary of the cash and demand deposits as of September 30, 19xx and 19xw:

	September 30,	
	19xx	*19xw*
Working cash funds	$ 1,000	$ 500
Office imprest cash fund	500	500
Demand deposits:		
Blank National Bank	35,500	21,600
Third National Bank	45,000	38,000
Total	$82,000	$60,600

Note: *If there were any unusual circumstances in regard to the cash accounts, a description or comment would be put in at this point.*

Trade Accounts Receivable

Statements of account were sent to all customers showing balances as of September 30, 19xx, requesting that they notify us if the amount shown to be due was not correct. No unexplained differences were reported to us. Following is a summary of accounts receivable at September 30, 19xx and 19xw:

	19xx		*19xw*	
Month of Sale	*Amount*	*Per Cent*	*Amount*	*Per Cent*
September	$ 71,822	57.1	$70,291	77.5
August	7,184	5.7	10,158	11.2
July	9,217	7.3	3,355	3.7
Prior	37,597	29.9	6,872	7.6
Total	$125,820	100.0	$90,676	100.0

It was noted that through November 30, 19xx, the sum of $74,520 was collected on these accounts.

The Corporation was on a charge-off basis for bad debts, and all accounts which are doubtful of collection, in the opinion of management, have been charged off. Bad debts charged off for the year ended September 30, 19xx amounted to $1,429. This compares with a net bad debt expense for the previous year of $1,714.

Note: *Any special information in regard to accounts receivable or bad debts would be placed here. For example, if a material amount of the receivables were owed by a single customer, it would be so noted.*

Other Receivables

The Balance Sheet item captioned "Other Receivables" comprises the following:

Travel advances	$ 2,550
Advances to employees	5,900
Claims receivable for losses in shipment	7,300
Real estate tax refund, approved but not yet received	9,940
Total	$25,690

Note: *With many small and medium-sized businesses, "Other Receivables" are either too small, or are self- explanatory, so that there is no necessity for a special paragraph in the additional information section.*

Inventories

On September 29 and 30, 19xx, employees of the Company made a physical count of all items of inventory on hand, at which time our representatives were present and made tests of the count and description of the items. Purchased items are valued at invoice cost plus incoming freight, and manufactured items are valued at costs shown by the Company's cost system on a first-in, first-out basis. We have reviewed the cost system, and determined that it represents the actual average cost for the year ended September 30, 19xx. All damaged, obsolete, or unsalable merchandise has been priced at net salvage value.

Presented below is a summary of the inventory at September 30, 19xx and 19xw:

	September 30,	
	19xx	*19xw*
Raw material	$100,000	$ 50,000
Material in process	50,000	50,000
Finished goods	120,000	160,000
Purchased goods	33,500	26,900
Total	$303,500	$286,900

There has been no change in method of valuing inventories during the two fiscal years.

Note: *Had there been any change in valuing or counting the inventory, it would have been fully explained. Also, had there been any substantial change in the products manufactured or sold, a full explanation would be made.*

Prepaid Expenses

The amount of prepaid expenses shown on the balance sheet in the amount of $12,550 comprise the following items:

Prepaid and unexpired insurance	$ 5,560
Prepaid interest	4,990
Prepaid advertising	2,000
Total	$12,550

Note: *The above illustrates only those prepaid items comprising current assets; noncurrent prepaid assets would be shown similarly in the noncurrent portion of the Balance Sheet. This is fully explained in Chapter 7. In many instances, the amount of prepaid items is so small that it need not be listed in the supplemental information section.*

Fixed Assets and Accumulated Depreciation

Fixed assets are valued at cost. Depreciation is computed by straight-line and declining-balance methods. The amount so computed for the fiscal year ended September 30, 19xx is as follows:

Straight line	$20,000
Declining balance	32,600
Total	$52,600

Generally speaking, buildings and building equipment are depreciated by the straight-line method, and equipment by the declining-balance method. If the straight-line method had been used for equipment, the amount of depreciation expense for the fiscal year ended September 30, 19xx would have been approximately $12,000 less, and the net income, after income taxes, would have been approximately $6,000 greater.

The company routinely leases certain equipment, especially automobiles and trucks. None of these leases are for more than three years, and none provide for ultimate purchase.

Note: *Comments are advisable if depreciation methods other than straight-line ones are used, unless the amount is insignificant. If there are leases in effect which are the equivalent of purchase, they must be segregated and shown separately, as outlined in Chapter 8.*

Other Assets

The amount of $10,500 shown on the balance sheet as "Other Assets" comprises the following:

Cash guaranty deposits with utilities	$ 2,500
Covenant not to compete, amount to be written off after one year	6,000

Goodwill	2,000
Total	$10,500

The amount represented by covenant not to compete and goodwill arose through the purchase of the assets of the JKL Company in 19ww.

Note: *In many small and medium-sized businesses, Other Assets are too small to warrant special treatment. However, if they are significant, the foregoing may be used as an example of the method of presentation.*

Notes Payable

All notes, mortgages, contracts, and other negotiable instruments due at the audit date were confirmed by direct correspondence with the holders thereof. No differences were reported to us. As of September 30, 19xx, it appeared that all obligations were being paid as agreed and no delinquencies were noted.

Following is a detail of notes payable:

Mortgage payable—Life Insurance Company	$100,000
Portion due within one year	12,000
Secured by first mortgage on land and buildings, payable $1,000 per month plus interest on the unpaid balance at the rate of 6% per annum	
Note payable—Blank National Bank	25,000
Unsecured, due December 1, 19xx	
Contract payable—Blank National Bank	3,600
Portion due within one year	1,200
Secured by GMC truck, payable $100 per month, interest included	
Summary:	
Notes payable—current portion	$38,200
Notes payable—deferred	90,400
Total	$128,600

Note: *There are several ways in which the foregoing information could be presented. If there are numerous notes, it may be more convenient to prepare a separate schedule. Figure 16-1 (page 208, 209) illustrates such a schedule. It is very important to indicate the time that payments are to be made, so that a budget can be prepared. While the security, if any, will necessarily be shown on the balance sheet or in accompanying notes to financial statements, it is advisable to repeat and to detail this information, so that it can be related to the specific payable.*

X Y Z COMPANY

NOTES AND MORTGAGES PAYABLE

SEPTEMBER 30, 19XX

	Collateral
John and Mary Smith	First mortgage on land and buildings located at 9999 West 99 Avenue, Our Town, State.
Blank National Bank and Small Business Administration, an agency of the United States Government	All land (subject to above first mortgage), buildings, equipment, autos, trucks, assignment of life insurance policies.
Blank National Bank (90% guaranteed by the Small Business Administration)	All land, buildings, equipment, autos, trucks, assignment of life insurance policies subject to first mortgage, above.
Third National Bank	Accounts receivable.
John Doe	None *
Richard Doe	None *
Mary Doe	None *
J K L Corporation	None *
I N M Insurance Company	Casualty insurance policies.

* Payment of principal is subordinated to payment of loans to the Blank National Bank and the Small Business Administration.

Figure 16-1

Date of Loan	Amount of Original Loan	Balance September 30, 19xx	Rate of Interest	Due Within One Year	Due After One Year	Interest Accrued to September 30, 19xx
2-23-VV	$155,000	$ 80,000	5%	$12,000	$ 68,000	$ 200
3-31-VV	68,750	40,000	7%	6,000	34,000	300
3-31-VV	206,250	120,000	5½%	20,000	100,000	600
5-25-XV	50,000	40,000	7%	40,000	. . . . . .	100
12-15-XV	60,000	60,000	6%	. . . . .	60,000	. . .
12-15-XV	40,000	40,000	6%	. . . . .	40,000	500
12-15-XV	7,000	7,000	6%	. . . . .	7,000	100
12-15-XV	7,500	7,500	6%	. . . . .	7,500	. . .
10- 1-XW	6,000	4,718	Included	4,718	. . . . . .	. . .
		$399,218		$82,718	$316,500	$1,800

Figure 16-1 (contd.)

Trade Accounts Payable

Vendor's statements, invoices, and other data were examined to the extent deemed appropriate, and in addition, a request was sent to all creditors showing a balance due of $100 or more, asking that they confirm directly to us the amount due at the balance sheet date. No differences were reported. An aging of the accounts payable is presented below:

| | September 30, | | | |
| | 19xx | | 19xw | |
Invoiced in:	Amount	%	Amount	%
September	$106,373	57.3	$30,580	91.6
August	33,498	18.0	—	—
July	35,942	19.3		
Prior	9,935	5.4	2,800	8.4
Total	$185,748	100.0	$33,380	100.0

The amount of $9,935 shown as invoiced prior to July, 19xx, represents a disputed item due to FGH and Company, arising through the shipment of defective merchandise. While the exact amount which will ultimately be paid on this account is not determinable at this time, the figure of $9,935 denotes the maximum liability to the Corporation.

Note: *The aging of the accounts payable indicates how well the company is meeting its trade obligations, and is valuable information for the credit grantor. Any special information regarding accounts payable should be commented upon. For example, if a large portion of the accounts payable is due to one creditor, this should be noted.*

Other Liabilities

The amount of $20,250 shown on the Balance Sheet as "Accrued Taxes" consists of the following:

Accrued FICA taxes	$ 1,500
Accrued federal income taxes withheld	2,500
Accrued federal unemployment tax	3,250
State unemployment tax	4,000
State sales tax	9,000
Total	$20,250

Note: *A detail listing of accrued taxes and/or expenses would be made only if sufficient detail were not on the balance sheet itself and the amount large enough to justify its inclusion in this section.*

Income Taxes Payable

We reviewed the computation of the federal and state income taxes for the fiscal year ended September 30, 19xx. The amount shown on the Balance Sheet represents the balance due for the fiscal year then ended. It was noted that agents of the Internal Revenue Service have examined the Corporation's income tax returns through the year ended September 30, 19vv. No tax deficiencies were assessed. The state income tax returns have not been examined for the past three years.

Note: *The latest years for which federal and state (if any) income tax returns have been examined should always be indicated.*

Stockholders' Equity

The amount of $15,000 shown on the Balance Sheet as "Contributed Surplus" arose from the sale of treasury stock for an amount in excess of its cost to the Corporation.

Note: *Details of most of the items making up stockholders' equity will necessarily appear on the balance sheet or on notes to financial statements. In the event that there should be any items not fully described therein, they should be listed in the supplemental information section. It should be noted that in this illustration, a list of stockholders was included immediately following the list of officers. It could equally well be shown under "Stockholders' Equity."*

Insurance

The following insurance policies were submitted for our inspection, and are listed for information only. We have not audited the insurance coverage, nor have we verified that the policies listed are in force. It was noted that there does not appear to be a fidelity bond in force.

Policy Number	Carrier	Peril	Amounts (in $M)	Property Insured
ABC-12345	LMN Ins. Co.	Fire-e/c	500	Buildings contents
9876-22	GHI Cas. Co.	Liability prop. damage	300/500	General liability
X-444-yz	PQR Ins. Co.	Cargo damage	10	All cargo in transit
B-678-M	PQR Ins. Co.	Burglary	10	Enclosed premises

Note: *A listing of the insurance policies in effect is useful information, since it may call attention to any coverage which may have been overlooked. Unless special arrangements have been made, an audit of the insurance policies is not a part of normal audit procedures and it should be clearly indicated that they are listed for convenience, and have not been audited.*

STYLE MANUAL

Every magazine and newspaper and most large business organizations have some type of an instructional manual for the preparation of correspondence, memoranda, reports, and the like. The purpose of the manual is to provide instructions in the proper handling of format, of punctuation, of spelling (when more than one form is acceptable), the type of paper to be used, method of reproduction in the event that more than one copy will be required, and generally to provide a source of information for the guidance of both old and new employees. Without such a manual consistency would be impossible, since no one can remember exactly from time to time how such clerical details are to be handled.

Although most of the larger accounting firms have such a manual, in a more or less elaborate form, many smaller accounting firms have failed to take advantage of this device. The style manual, often called "Office Manual," "Report Manual," "Clerical Guide," or by some similar name, is most useful in writing reports. The desired form of salutation, of content, and such minor but quite important details appearing on the financial statement as the number and position of dollar signs, when words are to be capitalized, the use of punctuation, and other items which are a necessary mechanical part of each financial statement, are indicated.

In many accounting organizations there is one experienced statistical typist who has, over a period of time, learned from the partners and supervisors the form in which financial statements and reports are desired. Accordingly, she is able to type from rough draft and produce a finished report in exact accordance with the policy of the firm.

Unfortunately, however, it is not always possible to have such a person do all of the typing and provision must necessarily be made for absences and changes in personnel. Also, new staff members are entitled to have some guidance as to the form in which the firm expects to have the final report prepared. Accordingly, no matter how small the office, such an office manual should be established and maintained. It need not be elaborate, and often one copy may suffice for a small office. Since every office has some type of copying equipment, the problem of supplying sufficient copies of a style manual is a very simple one. As a word of caution, however, one member of the organization should be given the responsibility of maintaining and supervising such a manual. Failure to do this will result in changes being made in one copy and not being properly changed in all, with the result that consistency, which is the objective of the style manual in the first place, is defeated.

The manual, in addition to stating what should be included, is often used to indicate words and expressions which should be avoided. Captions used on financial statements are largely a matter of personal preference, at least within a general range, but one firm may object to the use of captions commonly used by another. For example, the term "cash" is found frequently in balance sheets. It is understood that this does not mean literally currency or silver, but is used to indicate in addition money held in banks. Literally, "cash in banks" is somewhat of a misnomer, since obviously the auditor has no way of knowing that these particular funds are actually in the bank in the form of currency, and what is actually meant usually is "demand deposits." However, taken in the broader sense, the term "cash" on a balance sheet is understood to mean "cash on hand" and "demand deposits." Various accounting firms have their own personal preference as to which they use. The exact terminology is probably not too important, providing always that it conforms with acceptable usage.

The style manual offers an excellent opportunity to include a list of balance sheet, income account, retained earnings and statement of source, and application of funds captions which are to be used under normal circumstances.

The use of terminology in financial statements as well as in auditor's reports is one that is continually changing. When a manual has been put into use, it should not, therefore, be completely ignored but reviewed and updated from time to time, in order that the financial statements and reports issued by the firm will be in accordance with the most acceptable terminology.

A well-written and carefully reproduced report, based upon sound auditing procedures will fulfill the auditor's obligation to his client, to the public, and to his fellow practitioners.

Index

A

Abstracts, 43
Accounting Principles Board of the American Institute of Certified Public Accountants, 107
Accounts payable, trade, 113–142 (*see also* Trade accounts payable)
Accounts receivable, 64–65
Accrued taxes:
  audit program, 148
  categories, 143
  financial statement presentation, 154–157
    contingent liabilities, 156–157
    expenses, 156
    income taxes, 155
    other taxes, 156
    supplemental information, 155
  general outline of accrued expenses, 145
  reserves, 145–147
    against debt, 146
    asset revaluation, 145
    contingent liabilities for leases, service contracts, etc., 147–148
    indicate liability, 146–147
    surplus, 145–146
  special situations, 154
  verification, 151–154
    contingent liabilities, 154
    excise taxes, 153
    income taxes, 152
    licenses and fees, 153
    payroll taxes, 151
    property taxes, 153
    sales taxes, 152–153
    withheld taxes, 152
  working papers, 148, 150–151
    contingent liabilities, 151
    expenses, 151

Accrued taxes (contd.)
  income taxes payable, 148, 150
  other taxes, 150–151
  payroll taxes, 149
  withheld taxes, 148
"Administrative" expense, 179
Advances, officers and employees, 98, 101
Adverse opinion, **193**
Advertising expense, 184, 187–188
Amortization, expense accounts, 186, 187
Analyzing Financial Statements, 23, 24
"Anticipation," 172
Asset revaluation, 145
Assignment letter:
  example, 35–36
  no particular form, 35
  restrictions, 34
  value and content, 34
Auditor:
  judged, 36
  opinion, 191–198 (*see also* Opinion of auditor)
  report, 199–213 (*see also* Report of auditor)
  responsibility, 23, 25–28, 34
    assignment letter, 34
    cognizance of information required, 23
    express professional opinion, 25
    prepare report properly, 23
    standards, auditing, 25–28
  verification of inventories, 79

B

Bad debt reserve, 65, 70
Bank reconciliation, 58, 60
Benefit plans, 22
Bonding system, 51
Bonds, 120–121
"Bonus depreciation," 106

Borrowing, 50
Bureau of Labor Statistics Price Index, 90
"Buy-sell" agreement, 22

C

C, 44
Cancelled checks, compare, 60, 61
Capital accounts:
    business organization, types, 159–160
        corporation, 159–160
        estate, 160
        joint venture, 159–160
        partnership, 159–160
        proprietorship, 159
        syndicate, 159–160
        trust, 160
    financial statement presentation, 165–166
    program, audit, 160–161
        corporation, 160–161
        partnership, 160
        sole proprietorship, 160
        subsequent to audit date, 160–161
    verification, 162–164
        capital accounts, 162
        capital contributions, 164
        capital stock, 162–163
        nonprofit organizations, 164–165
        other surplus accounts, 164
        retained earnings, 163–164
    working papers, 160–162
        capital accounts, 161
        capital stock accounts, 161
        other surplus accounts, 162
        retained earnings, 161–162
Capital asset, what constitutes, 106
Capital gains, special tax treatment, 168
Cash:
    audit program, 56–57
        prior to audit date, 56
        subsequent to audit date, 56–57
    financial statement presentation, 61–62
    receipts, 55
    special situations, 61
    unauthorized uses, 55
    use of term, 55
    verification, 60–61
        cancelled checks, 61
        cash in bank, 60–61
    working papers required, 57–60
        cash count, 57
        compare cancelled checks, 60
        comparison of recorded cash receipts and bank
            deposits, 57–58
        prove footings and trace postings, 60
        reconcile bank accounts, 58, 60
        verification of journal entries, 60
"Cash on hand and in the banks," 61, 62

Cash registers, 51
Casualty and theft losses, 188
Change funds, 62
Chattel mortgage, 119
Commissions, 181
Computers, 51
Conditional sales contract, 120
Consigned inventories, 86–87, 89
"Consolidated," use of word, 175
Consumer paper, 50
Contingent liabilities, 147–148, 151, 154, 156–157
Contractors, 75–76
Contracts receivable, 65
Contributions, expense accounts, 186, 187
Copying machines, 43–44
Copyrights, 102
Corporation, 159–160
Covers, working papers, 39
Credit, securing, 22–24, 36

D

Data-control devices, 51
Debt expense, bad, 185, 187
Deficiencies, letter outlining, 50
"Demand deposits," 61
Department stores, 89
Depletion, expense accounts, 186, 188
Deposits, 95, 100
Depreciation, fixed assets:
    accumulated, 112
    allowance, 109, 112
    expense account, 186, 187
    summary, 112
    20 per cent "bonus depreciation," 106
Development expenses, deferred, 98
Dictating equipment, 43–44
Disclaimer of opinion, 193
Dividends received, 168, 170, 172
Drafts, notes payable, 119–120

E

Employees, advances, 98, 101
Endorsement, fraudulent or erroneous, 50
Entertainment expenses, 181, 188
Estate, 160
Estate planning, 22
Excise taxes, 143, 144, 153
Expense accounts:
    advertising, 184
    amortization, 186
    audit program, 186
    bad debt expense, 185
    categories, 179
    commissions, 181
    contributions, 186
    cost of sales, 180–181

Expense accounts (contd.)
  depletion, 186
  depreciation, 186
  entertainment, 181
  financial statement presentation, 189–190
  interest, 186
  labor, 180
  rent, 185
  repairs, 185
  special situations, 189
  taxes, 184
  travel, 181
  verification, 189
  working papers, 186–189
    advertising, 187–188
    bad debts, 187
    casualty and theft losses, 188
    contributions, 187
    depletion, 188
    depreciation and amortization, 187
    entertainment, 188
    extraordinary and nonrecurring expenses, 189
    insurance, 188
    interest, 187
    officer's salaries, 186–187
    professional fees, 188–189
    rents, 187
    repairs, 187
    taxes, 188
Expenses:
  accrued, 151, 156
  prepaid, 93–104 (see also Prepaid expenses)
Experimental expenses, 103
Extensions, 86

F

Federal income tax returns, 107
Field work, standards, 25, 28–36, 37, 44
Filing, working papers, 40
Financial organizations, 75
Financial statement presentation:
  accrued taxes, 154–157
  capital accounts, 165–166
  cash, 61–62
  disclosures, 193
  expense accounts, 189–190
  fixed assets, 115–116
  income accounts, 175–177
  inventories, 90–91
  notes payable, 129–131
  prepaid expenses, 103–104
  receivables, 76–77
  report of auditor, 201
  trade accounts payable, 141
Fixed assets:
  audit program, 107–108
    prior to audit date, 107

Fixed assets (contd.)
    subsequent audit date, 107–108
  detailed ledger, 106
  federal income tax returns, 107
  financial statement presentation, 115–116
  importance varies, 105
  number of ways to keep record, 105–106
  reasons to maintain detailed records, 106
  special situations, 112, 115
  20 per cent "bonus depreciation," 106
  verification, 112
    accumulated depreciation, 112
    assets, 112
  what constitutes capital asset, 106
  working papers, 108–112
    allowance for depreciation, 109, 112
    current audit file, 109
    permanent file, 108
    summary of depreciation, 112
Footings, 60, 86
Franchised businesses, 22
Fraud, 50

G

Gains from sale of fixed assets and investments, 168, 170
"General expense," 179
Goodwill, 98, 102

H

Headings, working papers, 40–41

I

Imprest cash funds, 62
Income accounts:
  "anticipation," 172
  audit program, 169
  categories, 167
  extraordinary income, 168
  incidental income, 167
  mercantile business, 167–168
  "nonrecurring income," 168
  "regular income," 167
  requiring special auditing, 168
  service organization, 167
  special situations, 174–175
  verification, 170, 172–174
    dividends, 172
    interest, 173
    net gains and losses, 173
    other income, 174
    rents, 173
    royalties, 173
    two categories, 170
  working papers, 170

Income accounts (contd.)
    dividends, 170
    gains and losses, 170
    interest, 170
    other income, 170
    rents, 170
    royalties, 170
Income taxes, 143, 144, 148, 150, 152, 155
Indexing, working papers, 41–43
Insurance:
  expense accounts, 188
  life, cash value, 99–100
  unexpired, 94–95, 99
Interest:
  expense accounts, 186, 187
  income accounts, 168, 170, 173
Internal control:
  amount necessary, 49–50
  basic principle, 46
  bonding system, 51
  borrowings, 50
  cash and receivables, 50
  cash registers, 51
  client's representations, 51–53
    combining two "Certificates," 53
    Inventory Certificate, 51–52
    Liability Certificate, 52
  computers, 51
  consumer paper, 50
  data-control devices, 51
  defined, 45
  fraudulent or erroneous endorsement, 50
  "lapping," 50
  letter outlining deficiencies, 50
  machine bookkeeping, 51
  mechanical devices, 51
  questionnaire, 46–49
    advantage, 46
    personnel, letters indicating, 49
    suggested basic form, 47–49
    use, 46–47
  second standard of field work, 45
  system, examination, 46
  two or more people, 46
  type of business, 49–50
In-transit items, 86
Inventories:
  audit program, 80–83
    as of audit date, 82
    prior to audit date, 80–81
    subsequent to audit date, 82–83
  computing during fiscal year, 80
  department stores, 89
  financial statement presentation, 90–91
  instructions for count, 81
  perpetual method, 90
  retail businesses, 89
  significance as portion of total current assets, 79

Inventories (contd.)
  special situations, 89–90
  three general categories,79
    manufacturer's, 79
    retail, 79
    wholesale, 79
  verification, 87–89
    consigned inventory, 87, 89
    finished goods, 87
    purchased material, 87
    work in process, 87
  warehouses, materials in, 89
  working papers, 83–87
    consigned inventories, 86–87
    cost, extensions, footings, 86
    count, 83–84
    instructions, copy, 84
    in-transit items, 86
    last invoice, 86
    last receiving report, 86
    summary, 87
Inventory Certificate, 51–52
Inventory count, 83, 84
Invoice, last, 86

J

Job order number, 84
Joint venture, 159–160

L

Labor expense, 180
"Lapping," 50
Leases, contingent liabilities, 147–148
Letter outlining deficiencies, 50
Liabilities, contingent, 147–148, 151, 154, 156–157
Liability Certificate, 52
Losses from sale of fixed assets and investments, 168, 170

M

Machine bookkeeping, 51
Manual on preparing working papers, 38–44
Master time schedule, 33–34
Mechanical devices, 51
Microphone, neck, 44

N

Nonprofit organization, purposes of audit, 24
Notes payable:
  audit program, 121
    as of audit date, 121
    subsequent to audit date, 121
  categories, 119–120
    bonds, 120–121

Notes payable (contd.)
    conditional sales contract, 120
    drafts, 119–120
    secured, 119
    unsecured, 119
  definition, 119
  detail, 131
  financial statement presentation, 129–131
  personalty, 119
  realty, 119
  special situations, 128–129
  verification, 122–123, 128
  working papers, 121–122
    current audit file, 122
    permanent file, 121–122
    trial balance, 122
Notes receivable:
  verification, 72–74
  working papers, 65

O

Officers, advances, 98, 101
Opinion of auditor:
  adverse, 193
  disclaimer of opinion, 193
  events subsequent to audit date, 197
  qualified, 193
  scope of audit, 195–197
    circumstances beyond control, 195
    restrictions imposed by client, 195
  "standard short form report," 193
    auditor's signature, 193
    date, 193
    expository paragraph, 193–194
    opinion paragraph, 193, 194
    salutation, 193
    sample, 194
  standards of reporting, 191
    first, 191–192
    fourth, 193
    second, 192
    stated, 191
    third, 192–193
  unaudited statements, 198
  unqualified, 193
Organization expense, 98, 101–102

P

Paper:
  consumer, 50
  size, 38–39
  stock, 39
Part number, 84
Partnership, 159–160
Patents, 98, 102
Payroll taxes, 143, 149, 151

Perpetual inventory method, 90
Personalty, 119
Photocopy, 43
Postings, trace, 60
Prepaid expenses:
  audit program, 64
  financial statement presentation, 103–104
  special situations, 103
  verification, 99–103
    advances to employees, 101
    advances to officers, 101
    cash value of life insurance, 99–100
    deposits, 100
    goodwill, 102
    organization expense, 101–102
    patents, copyrights, trademarks, 102
    prepaid expenses, 100
    research and experimental expenses, 103
    unexpired insurance, 99
  working papers, 94–99
    advances to employees, 98
    advances to officers, 98
    cash value life insurance, 95
    covenant not to compete, 98
    deferred research and development expenses, 98
    deposits, 95
    goodwill, 98
    organization expense, 98
    others, 99
    patents, 98
    prepaid expenses, 95
    trademarks, 98
    unexpired insurance, 94–95
Preprinted work sheets, 39
Professional fees, 188–189
Profit organization, purposes of audit, 21–24
Program:
  accrued taxes, 148
  basic outline, 29–32
  capital accounts, 160–161
  cash, 56–57
  defined, 28–29
  discussion of primary purpose, 34
  expense accounts, 186
  fixed assets, 107–108
  function, 29
  income accounts, 169
  inventories, 80–83
  master time schedule, 33–34
  notes payable, 121
  prepaid expenses, 94
  receivables, 64
  trade accounts payable, 134–135
Property Taxes, 143, 144, 153
Proprietorship, 159
Purposes of audit:
  discussion to establish, 34
  nonprofit organizations, 24

Purposes of audit (contd.)
    profit organization, 21–24
        advice and counsel, 23
        benefit plans, 22
        estate planning, 22
        franchised businesses, 22
        many states, 21
        sale of business, 22
        securing credit, 22–24, 36
        two or more interests involved, 21

Q

Qualified opinion, 193
Questionnaire, internal control, 46–49

R

Realty, 119
Receivables:
    audit program, 64
        as of audit date, 64
        subsequent to audit date, 64
    financial statement presentation, 76–77
    special situations, 75–76
        contractors, 75–76
        financial organizations, 75
        service organizations, 75
        utilities, 76
    verification, 70–74
        notes receivable, 72–74
        trade accounts receivable, 70–72
    working papers required, 64–65, 70
        accounts receivable, 64–65
        bad debts reserve, 65, 70
        contracts receivable, 65
        notes receivable, 65
        other, 65
        write-off, 65, 70
Receiving report, last, 86
Recording device, 44
Rent:
    expense accounts, 185, 187
    income accounts, 168, 170, 173
Repairs, cost, 185, 187
Report of auditor:
    adequate checking, 199, 200
    assets and liabilities, 203
        assets, other, 206–207
        cash on hand and in banks, 203–204
        fixed assets and accumulated depreciation, 206
        income taxes payable, 211
        insurance, 211
        inventories, 205
        liabilities, other, 210
        notes and mortgages payable, 208–209
        notes payable, 207
        prepaid expenses, 205–206

Report of auditor (contd.)
        receivables, other, 205–206
        stockholders' equity, 211
        trade accounts payable, 210
        trade accounts receivable, 204
    commercial printer, 199
    comparative statements, 202–203
    contents, 199
    electrostatic machines, 199
    financial analyses, 202
    financial statement presentation, 201
    history of client, 200–201
    language, 200–201
    meticulously prepared, 199
    "Notes," 201
    offset press, 199
    organization of company, 202
    paper, letterhead, binding, 200
    physical appearance, 199
    Report Instructions Form, 200
    results of operations, 202
    simple arithmetical mistakes, 199
    style manual, 212–213
    supplemental information section, 201
    typographical errors, 199
    unusual occurrences, 203
    work papers, 200
Research and experimental expenses, 103
Research expenses, deferred, 98
Reserves, accrued taxes, 145–147 (*see also* Accrued taxes)
Responsibility of auditor, 23, 25–28, 34 (*see also* Auditor)
Retail businesses, 89
Retention, working papers, 40
"Revenue," service organization, 176
Royalties, income accounts, 168, 170, 173

S

Sales:
    cost, 180–181
    manufacturing or mercantile firm, 176
Sales taxes, 143, 144, 152, 153
Secured notes payable, 119
Service contracts, 147–148
Service organizations, 75
Sheet number, 84
Situations, special (*see* Special situations)
Special situations:
    accrued taxes, 154
    capital accounts, 164–165
    cash, 61
    expense accounts, 189
    fixed assets, 112, 115
    income accounts, 174–175
    inventories, 89–90
    notes payable, 128–129

Special situations (contd.)
    prepaid expenses, 103
    receivables, 75–76
    trade accounts payable, 140–141
"Standard short form report," 193 (see also Opinion of auditor)
Standards, auditing, 25–28
Style manual, 212–213
"Subchapter S corporation," 169
Symbols, auditing, 44
Syndicate, 159–160

T

Tag number, 84
Taxes:
    accrued, 143–157 (see also Accrued taxes)
    income, 184, 185
    licenses, permits, fees, 184, 185
    payroll, 184
    property, 184, 185
    sales and use, 184–185
Theft losses, casualty and, 188
"Tick" marks, 44
Time schedule, master, 33–34
Timesavers, 43–44
Trade accounts payable:
    audit program, 134–135
      as of audit date, 135
      prior to audit date, 134
      subsequent to audit date, 135
    confirmation, 133
    definition, 133
    financial statement presentation, 141
    first audit, 134
    problem for auditor, 134
    size, quantity, and type, 133
    special situations, 140–141
      concealed accounts payable, 140
      eliminating conspiracy, 140–141
    verification, 138–140
    working papers, 135
Trade accounts receivable, 70–72
Trademarks, 98, 102
Travel expenses, 181
Trust, 160
Trust indenture, 119

U

Ultramares, 25
Unqualified opinion, 193
Unsecured notes payable, 119
Utilities, 76

V

V, 44
Verification:
    accrued taxes, 151–154
    capital accounts, 162–164
    cash, auditing, 60–61
    expense account, 189
    fixed assets, 112
    income accounts, 170, 172–174
    inventories, 87–89
    journal entries, 60
    notes payable, 122–123, 128
    prepaid expenses, 99–103
    receivables, 70–74
    trade accounts payable, 138–140

W

Withheld taxes, 143, 144, 148, 152
Working papers:
    abstracts, 43
    accrued taxes, 148, 150–151
    capital accounts, 161–162
    cash, auditing, 57–60
    copying machine, 43–44
    covers, 39
    dictating equipment, 43–44
    evidence in court case, 37
    expense account, 186–189
    filing, 40
    fixed assets, 108–112
    forms, size and kind, 38
    headings, 40–41
    income accounts, 170
    indexing, 41–43
    inventories, 83–87
    manual on preparation, 38–44
    microphone, neck, 44
    notes payable, 121–122
    paper size, 38–39
    paper stock, 39
    prepaid expenses, 94–99
    preparation, 37–44
    preprinted work sheets, 39
    receivables, 64–65, 70
    recording device, 44
    retention, 40
    symbols, auditing, 44
    technical requirements, 38–44
    timesaving possibilities, 43–44
    trade accounts payable, 135
Write-off, 65, 70